"Rising from the Ashes of Divorce is the definitive book for surviving and thriving through your divorce - and beyond. It will affirm and enhance your life on every level: spiritual, emotional, social and financial. A MUST read for absolutely everyone going through a divorce."

Kathleen McGowan, NY Times Bestselling author of
The Expected One and The Source of Miracles

"Beth Tiger's book is food for the soul. Each word, each sentence was a guide to light my path through the darkness of divorce and over the mountain to a new way of life. Truly humanly lived and God inspired."

Betsy Moltane, Divorcee, Flying Solo Series participant

Rising from the Ashes of Divorce

Rising from the Ashes of Divorce

Book 1 of the
Flying Solo Series

Beth Tiger

BALBOA
PRESS

A DIVISION OF HAY HOUSE

ISBN: 978-1-4525-4615-5 (sc)
ISBN: 978-1-4525-4616-2 (e)
ISBN: 978-1-4525-4614-8 (hc)

Library of Congress Control Number: 2012905862

Balboa Press books may be ordered through booksellers or by contacting:

Balboa Press
A Division of Hay House
1663 Liberty Drive
Bloomington, IN 47403
www.balboapress.com
1-(877) 407-4847

Because of the dynamic nature of the Internet, any web addresses or links contained in this book may have changed since publication and may no longer be valid. The views expressed in this work are solely those of the author and do not necessarily reflect the views of the publisher, and the publisher hereby disclaims any responsibility for them.

The author of this book does not dispense medical advice or prescribe the use of any technique as a form of treatment for physical, emotional, or medical problems without the advice of a physician, either directly or indirectly. The intent of the author is only to offer information of a general nature to help you in your quest for emotional and spiritual well-being. In the event you use any of the information in this book for yourself, which is your constitutional right, the author and the publisher assume no responsibility for your actions.

Printed in the United States of America

Balboa Press rev. date:4/25/2012

Also by *Beth Tiger*,

Certified Life Coach

Rising from the Ashes of Divorce ~ the Course

A Weekend Retreat

A Life Well Lived

Center for Inspired Living

43 Spring Street

Ramsey, NJ 07446

For Apollo,
my loyal, gentle, loving Great Dane

He was by my feet
through the entire process of writing this book,
reminding me
of all the lessons
within these pages each day
with his unconditional love.

He was an inspiration in life,
and in spirit
he will forever be my guide.

Contents

Preface

As I begin on the journey of writing, I am in awe of the day before me. The rain has been unending, and there's been flooding in my area. It seems as though uprooted trees are everywhere. The weather has been humbling and out of control. However, as I type, the sun is coming out and the earth is drying. The air is sweet with the scent of flowers, and birds are singing to me.

I have often been amazed at what a paradox our lives are, much like the ways of nature. It is after intense weather that a rainbow appears or the plants and trees are able to blossom. Earth cleanses herself and starts fresh. Parts of her die, and others are born. It is during a forest fire that pinecones burst and their seeds are dispersed, offering the life-affirming regeneration the forest needs to sustain itself.

Living through the death of a marriage, separation and finally divorce is much the same. It's an arduous process, and for most of us, the loss feels like THE END, when in fact it is the beginning. For many of us, it is an unwanted beginning, but a beginning nonetheless. And like Earth, when humans are shaken to the core, we often get rid of things that no longer serve us. We discover a fresh perspective on our lives.

Some of us make the choice to divorce. For others, it comes as a complete surprise. Many of us experience it as a slow-growing cancer in our lives. In whatever way we reach a divorce, the process is often life draining, sad, lonely and scary, even if we know it is the right decision.

Divorce is change, and as creatures of habit we resist change, sometimes to the detriment of our minds, hearts and souls. The partner with whom we shared a life is gone, and life as we know it will never be the same. However, with the grace of God, just as Earth comes through a storm, we too come through the loss—oftentimes to our bewildered amazement. It is at this point, after the storm, that we are afforded the opportunity to bask in the light.

I ask you now . . . are you ready to walk deliberately into your life? Honoring all that you have been through with a forgiving and open heart? If the answer is yes to these questions, this workbook is for you.

Note that I said, "workbook." After the loss of a partner and the initial painful struggle, we think our work is done, but it is not.

Enjoying the gift of a beautiful garden is not a simple matter of planting new seeds. There is work to do. Our job is not to simply survive a storm; our work is to till the fertile, rich soil in the sacred garden of our limitless possibilities. It is through the daily care for the tender shoots that they become deeply rooted and begin to provide life-sustaining nutrition in the form of new perspectives, forgiveness, wondrous opportunities and love in all its forms.

That is the gift, given us by the Holy Spirit. After the hardship, we are offered the opportunity to thrive, not simply survive.

Acknowledgments

This book has taken me several years to finish, and I could not have completed it without the support of so many. For Joe and Ann McNulty, my wonderful parents: You are both living examples of enduring love. To my very large, imperfect, beautiful family, including but not limited to Laura Kirk; Joanne and Bob Hoertel; David and Laurie McNulty; Michael McNulty; Sean, Jennifer and Lauren Kirk; Jessica Hoertel, Erin Darvalics and Kate Lambrinides; Dan, Colleen and Rachel McNulty as well as Megan McNulty: All of you have been with me for the whole journey and for that I say, "Thank you."

To the "Transformation Crew," my first friend/soul family: You gave unconditional support and love during the trials of dating, marriage, divorce, re-marriage, etc. Thanks may have not always been expressed, but you were always appreciated. Thank the goddess you all love me :)

To my Mountain Rest, New Jersey, family: Thanks for teaching me it was OK to love again. Special acknowledgements to Bob Kohle, Jennifer Parette, Marc Parette, Heather O'Neil, Jennifer Harper and Jennifer Kania: Cheers! I also give thanks to God for introducing me to a special group of ladies that bring me closer to God and charity through our monthly SCC group and bring other women closer to spirit. They are Carol Williams, Liz Koch, Sue Furey, Linda Mamone and Susan Wright. Thank you for your enduring friendship. And thanks also to the past members, whom I will always cherish: Abigail Metzger and Margaret Pangert.

To my publicist, Mia Toschi: I feel especially blessed to be working alongside someone who shares my vision and hope for a better tomorrow through the Flying Solo program. To my editor, Jessica Cohn, thank you for bringing my message to life with such patience for this new author. For Dina Picciallo: You were an angel during the hardest transition of my life, and I will always be grateful. To my Sacred France spirit family and Kathleen and Filip: Thank you for demonstrating what a beautiful community could look and feel like; it gives me HOPE. A special thanks to Church of the Presentation in Upper Saddle River, New Jersey, for giving me a forum for the very first Flying Solo group. And for all the participants in the first few Flying Solo groups; you know who you are: Thank you for your honest sharing, love and beautiful wisdom. I learned so much alongside all of you. My prayer for each of you is that you have found peace, love and joy after the storm. To my three stepchildren, Timmy, Samantha and Katie: This road has been filled with twists and turns, but at the end of the day, love is the only thing that is real, and that is what is offered to each of you. A sincere thanks goes to Michael Alleva. Through our relationship, I learned what forgiveness really means for myself and those we love. I will always be grateful for our time together, all the lessons learned and the creation of our beautiful children. No regrets.

To the most important people in my life: God has richly blessed me by enriching my life through each of you. Though we may not have it all together, together we have it all! To my beautiful, amazing children, Jacob and Sam: Each day you teach me, love me and heal me. *Phew!* What more could a mom want? And to my beloved partner, Tim: Thank God for you. The time does return, and each day I give thanks for your unconditional love, support, friendship and passion. You are the song of my soul and a beautiful new chapter in the story that is my life.

Finally, the ultimate thanks goes to God, Easa, the Marys and the Holy Spirit for leading me through this process and life. Through God all things are possible. May all who read these pages be inspired and healed.

Namaste ~

Beth

Introduction

The Journey: Emotional and spiritual fulfillment after the loss of partnership through divorce

This book is an eight-week course, outlined in chapters 1 through 8; each section should be read and reflected on before moving to the next. The ninth chapter is for reflection. I have intentionally kept each chapter short because I believe that many of us get self-help books and after struggling through one long-winded chapter never read the rest. I would suggest that you take one chapter per week, re-reading it if you like, and use the question pages to journal your thoughts. Journaling our thoughts is a powerful tool. It aids us in our personal exploration and honors where we have been as well as where we are now. When we look back on our writing, it is like a map of where we were and where we wish to go.

I open each chapter with words of wisdom and end each chapter with prayer. Along the way, you'll find wonderful quotes from some of the most gifted visionaries of all time. In the prayers as well as when reading this book, feel free to substitute *God* for *Goddess, Great Spirit, Divine Intelligence* or whatever term brings the most comfort. As you will discover within these pages, one of the secrets, I feel, to moving forward in a positive direction is to deepen our connection to a power greater than ourselves and one another. By creating a more intimate relationship with this Source, our blinders are removed, and we are able to perceive our lives from a place of love and truth, trusting through faith that it is unfolding as it should, according to God's will.

At the end of each section, you will be given Divine Assignments to work through. I also pose a series of questions, which are great for inner reflection and also for conversation. They are meant to jump-start your heart and open the mind and psyche to your personal knowing. It is up to you how much you get out of this work—you will reap only what you sow—so put some overalls on, and let's get to it.

I love this quote by Thomas Edison: "Opportunity is missed by most people because it is dressed in overalls and looks like work." As a life coach, I know one thing for sure . . . within each of us is the capacity to create an amazing life. However, each of us must do this work for ourselves alone.

The Flying Solo Series is a celebration of resurrection and new life. What would the story of the crucifixion have meant if the resurrection had not occurred? No matter what your religious views are, most of us are familiar with the story. It is not the torture and death of Jesus that is the most important aspect but his ability to forgive those who hurt him and to rise from the fear and live again. It is the resurrection that is the miracle, and it is available to all of us if we choose it. It is our birthright as children of God to be reborn when the lives we are living no longer serve our highest purpose. All that you need for deep transformation, happiness and healing dwells within you.

God's essence is not in just some of us; it is in every being on this planet. There is no separation. That is and will always be the illusion of the ego. There is only connection through the unending love of God. This, dear friend, is the "Good News."

It is with a humble heart that I offer this program to you. Five years ago, I walked into Church of the Presentation in Upper Saddle River, New Jersey, not as a parishioner but as a divorced woman and life coach interested in sharing my coaching skills to the Divorce/Separated Ministry. I imagined speaking to the group for one evening. Short on volunteers, the pastoral director of the program asked if I would consider co-facilitating the program with other divorcées. At that point in my life, I felt so deeply blessed by all I had been through that I wanted to give back to others, so I said yes.

I worked alongside great individuals, who brought their own vulnerability to the program. Their generous spirit created the space for each participant to mourn, heal and grow through the difficult period of separation and divorce. It was a great experience.

When we were done with the sessions, the pastoral director asked me to create a program for people who were already divorced and still dealing with issues . . . a second step, so to speak. I jumped at the idea, putting all that I had gone through personally, and had been working on with my clients, to the test. I knew this was a gift from the Spirit. Yet at the time, I could not imagine the places it would take me both personally and professionally. It was in creating that eight-week program that *Rising from the Ashes of Divorce,* Book 1 of the Flying Solo Series, came to be.

An eight-week guide to creating a deliberate life

After the first eight-week session, I knew I had to create a workbook, but something stopped me from moving forward with that project immediately. With trust in God, I surrendered to the fact that I was stuck, so to speak, and would create the workbook on his time not mine.

The program evolved in the days and months that followed, as I witnessed how our group's members interacted. We were unified, through love or fear, and each individual, coming from one place or the other, became part of a collective whole. As I worked to help the members from a detached, loving place, it was amazing to hear the beautiful wisdom and insights that were expressed and see how, together, we were shifting from fear-based thought to thoughts of love.

It was true! Each of us had the answers within ourselves to lead our best lives. We just needed a safe space and time to simmer—to awaken the higher self and bring about our own personal transformations. I also came to understand that we all shared a deep longing for loving, nonjudgmental support and community; so not only was the Flying Solo Series created at the church, but a center for reflection and consideration was also manifested.

I look at this creation as a gift from Spirit. I am merely the messenger. There is only one truth but many messengers. I support you in exploring all types of study during this eight-week journey, which will inspire and uplift you. But I also implore you. Stay away from negative TV, tune out occasionally from the Internet, and take time for real person-to-person interaction. Listen to uplifting music; perhaps even pick a mantra that you will listen to every day to remind you of why you are doing this work. Hang positive affirmations on your wall, say the prayers offered in each chapter twice a day for the week you are working within the chapter, and most importantly, take time for nurturing yourself with a massage or some other form of bodywork or self-care routine; even a walk in the woods or time with your pet helps.

This eight-week journey is about healing your wounds so that you can celebrate the life you are living now. Although I am not with you in person, I am truly with you in spirit, and I honor each of you as you embark on your journey to live well, find love and create a deeper, more meaningful daily experience for yourself. May God bless each of you with a Life Well Lived. May it be yours.

Chapter 1

Learn the Lesson,
Lose the Story

My life has a superb cast but I can't figure out the plot.

~ Ashleigh Brilliant

When recalling the story of my marriage and subsequent divorce, I am aware of what a great, juicy story it was. There were villains and victims, knights and queens, and, of course, a fair maiden who needed to be saved from a cruel king.

I must state with total clarity that those were illusions. I created them in my mind to keep from looking honestly at my situation and blessing and releasing my inner quarrels with my ex-spouse. Of course, this is easy for me to write now, eight years later; if you had asked me about my marriage and the death of that union while I was going through my divorce, my story would have featured the maiden and other supporting characters.

Although I thought I was "owning" my part in the divorce, I most certainly was acting the part of the fair maiden, and my actions were merely reactions to my ex's supposed bad behavior. This wasn't clear to me until I started to study *A Course in Miracles* and many other beautiful pieces of modern and ancient spirituality. It was not until I truly got down on my knees and handed my life over to God that I began to see these patterns in my life.

I was introduced to a sacred prayer practice, which simplified my spirituality and brought me closer to God and my life's purpose than I ever dreamed possible. Before my resurrection, I had conversations filled with hate, shame, blame and anger, all of which kept me in a negative state of being, even on days that were brilliant and wonderful. The power of these emotions was continually pulling me toward the bottom.

It was too scary to even consider declaring that my life was not a fairy tale gone wrong but a blessed manifestation of God's love. It was frightening to think about what might happen if I tried looking at my relationship with my ex from a loving and forgiving place, so I held on tight to my old story until the day I finally decided to step into the fear and unleash these powerful changes of thought.

You know what occurred? A miracle! Not a metaphorical change but an honest-to-goodness miracle. My life was forever transformed and altered in ways I could never have even dreamed possible. It is because of this miracle, and the many since, that I want to share this work with you.

Miracles are our birthright, but we sit idly by, not expecting them to happen for us. Meanwhile, the Holy Spirit wants us to experience miracles on a daily basis because, in so doing, we gain a greater intimacy with God.

Are you ready for miracles in your life? Well, let's begin.

The price of anything is the amount of life you exchange for it.

~ Henry David Thoreau

It had been almost two years since my ex and I decided it was over, and we were in the throes of our divorce battle, sorting out financial matters, custody, homes, and a business. I was outraged and told my story to anyone who would listen; after all, it was a great tale.

When I told my story, people related to it, and they were angered and incensed by a situation about which they knew nothing firsthand. I realized then that we all love to meet each other in what I call our wounded place. It's like having a clubhouse where the wounded bring hankies and chocolate chip cookies to share. Looking back, I cringe to think about it, but at the time, who cared? I just wanted anyone to listen to my version of the facts.

In the early summer, during my divorce proceedings, I went away with my brother, who is a guardian angel in my life. We were sitting one evening in a beautiful field. I was in shock over a recent meeting with my soon-to-be ex's attorney and my lawyer. Of course, I was feeling like

3

the victim. My brother sat patiently, listening to my ranting about how I was being dealt another unfair deal. He lovingly allowed me to share my frustrations without interjecting or adding any fuel to my anger.

A sudden, miraculous thought came to me out of nowhere, and I said, "What if I stop the fighting and just settle? I will definitely not get what I feel I am entitled to financially, and I will be conceding to things that I may not feel are fair, but what if the fighting just stopped?"

He sat and was very quiet, and then said simply, "Yeah, that feels right." Nothing more. We sat for another minute, and it was in that simple moment that I experienced my first miracle.

There was no thunder boom or lightning bolt. No angel walked up to me and handed me the divine *How to Get Divorced* manual. Though it may sound crazy, my mind was simply and easily altered. My thoughts went from those of fear to those of love, and in that holy instant I was at peace.

Prior to that moment, I was fighting for things that in this world seem important: financial security, the well-being of my children, my home, an automobile. But I realized that if the battle continued, conflict would be all I attracted into my life and I would never be free from anger and fear.

I draw to me that which I am thinking, so by fighting, I was creating more anger and chaos around me. Was that good for my children? In fighting for financial resources, I was focusing on lack instead of future abundance and the possibilities in the present moment.

I have been asked over and over how we can truly change our minds. Though this transformation is so simple, it is something we resist. Really, what we focus on is what we create. In that moment with my brother, I finally surrendered. I unclenched my fists and considered for a moment what life would be like without a fight.

Ahh . . . what a nice thought.

In my life after divorce, I have had to remind myself on many occasions of that miracle. It is not as though I became completely Christ-like after that day; however, I do aspire to live my life in closer union with Spirit, and when I do have struggles with my ex, I can honestly say I try to see his perspective and act from love to the best of my current ability.

The experience with my brother gave me insight that I can always tap into. The saying "Once you know better, you do better" applies. I realize that today I can, quite simply, decide to be happy instead of right. I can end a fight. A miracle is always mine for the taking, as it is yours.

When we get caught up in our past stories, especially those filled with hate and blame, we are not fully alive. It is this moment that is the gift, and it is only in the present where we meet God. So no more meeting your friends at your wounded place. It serves no one, especially not you. For today, put the chocolate chip cookies away, and sit in the present moment with all of your feelings, considering what is next.

Life is not a fairy tale, and no one gets a pain-free pass. Now you get to author your story based on what you want, feel, and need, and you have the chance to fly freely—to soar. You are no longer co-author of one chapter of your life.

There is no past we can bring back by longing for it.

There is only an eternally new now that builds

and creates itself out of the best as the past withdraws.

~ Goethe

We share who we are with our stories. Our stories are critical in the telling of how we are evolving and growing. They offer us an opportunity to glimpse into the world of other people and places. As a species, it is through our oral and written traditions that we have come to know and understand our ancestors, various cultures, and religions as well as share in political, spiritual, and philosophical thought. It is from some of the most mystical stories that many of our world religions are based.

Unfortunately, history is often told as "his" story, and most times it is the story of the winner in a given situation. If we are to truly understand any situation or event, we must listen to the stories of at least three participants: the winner, the loser, and the objective observer. When we have not been given the whole story, we form opinions based on limited information.

For instance, when I grew up, I heard and saw movies in which American Indian nations were depicted as savage, ruthless, and cruel. I was taught that the Americas were discovered by Christopher Columbus, but how could that have been? Were not the Americas land that was already inhabited? I was also taught about the Pilgrims' flight from Europe because of religious persecution. I was told how kind the Indians were that first Thanksgiving; however, nothing was mentioned about the early settlers' intolerance toward Native American religion.

It was not until I was in my twenties that I began to read literature about the genocide of the Native Americans. I read and gained deeper understanding about their beautiful spirituality and the ways in which they honored Earth and all living things. My feelings went from fear and contempt to humility and awe. I was amazed at how my opinion could shift with more knowledge.

It was during this time that I also became aware of the awesome power of spell-casting—how with our words and stories we can sway others' opinions. I became acutely aware of the times when I discussed people, places, or situations, and my listeners acquired "their own" opinions based on what I said.

Unfortunately, this is a power that I have abused over time. I know that each of us has this power, and I challenge you from this day forth to use it with grace and integrity. When you talk about someone else, if you say negative things, ask yourself why you feel the need to discuss the person in this way.

So, what does this have to do with the story of your divorce? A LOT! Oftentimes, when we are hurting and angry it is through the tale of our broken relationships that we acquire allies. It is also my experience that in most stories of divorce, more often than not, the speaker is the person who was wronged.

Isn't it funny that it took two to fall in love, get married and be married but usually one person is to blame? Sure . . . we listen, oftentimes with deaf ears, to the coach or therapist who reminds us that it takes two, but when we are hurting we believe it has been all their fault, not ours.

I met with 12 participants in my first Flying Solo group and can report that they all felt as though they were the victims of their divorces. Even if one or two did the leaving, the story was that their marriages ended because the other person did this or that.

Why do we do this? It comes from being deeply wounded and vulnerable. It is also hard to look at the parts we played in the demise of our marriages. If we keep telling our stories and blaming our partners, even for our actions, we do not have to take responsibility. This means we do not have to sit in the shame or pain. Unfortunately, unless we own our piece, we will never move out of this place, and we will just keep repeating the same mistake.

I once heard a very wise woman quote scripture. She said, "Although I walk through the valley of death I will fear no evil." She said this to a group of divorcées, reminding them that the key was "walking through," not building a home or hanging out in the valley.

You do not get to transcend the experience of divorce. You must walk through the situation, be present in the pain and learn the lesson given to you. Once you do, you realize that you can walk through and survive, and from this vantage, you can live in the present. Owning mistakes becomes less scary.

It is important to remember that we change our minds or perspective at will. The cup half empty or half full is a great metaphor for this. When we are happy and thriving, we often see things from the cup half full perspective; when life becomes hard, we live in the perspective of the cup half empty.

Time is an aid for changing perspective. Circumstances change, and many wounds heal. But what if we consciously choose to change perspective now? When I hear people explaining why their marriages did not work out, as if that were the end of their story, I remember that they are under the influence of their current perspective. If I talk about the opportunities before them, because their circumstances have changed, it is amazing to see the shift in their perspective.

During divorce, we often vilify our spouses to protect our very fragile egos. It is because of the ego, though, that this state of fear exists. If we were coming from the perfect place within each of us, where the Divine dwells, we would see that we do not need others to be wrong in order for our feeling to be right. Our thoughts and feelings simply need to be in alignment with what we intuitively know is right for us. Period.

A Course in Miracles states that we either come from a place of love or fear. When we trash an ex-spouse, blaming him or her for the misery of our current reality, we are acting from fear. Fear of not being loveable, fear of the unknown, fear that we have no worth, fear there is not enough for us. However, in the eyes of God we are all miracles and deserve to be here. We are here not to perpetuate hate, but to experience love.

It is in our intimate relationships that we do our greatest learning. When we learn through fear, we often stay in relationships that no longer serve our or our partners' highest good. We are so afraid of moving forward that we hold on to things that are no longer in our best interest to have. Unfortunately, this can be very painful, and many of us have experienced this kind of hurt deep within our souls. Once again, it is our fear of being unlovable that many times keeps us in situations that devastate our self-worth and perpetuate this state of fear.

In three words I can sum up everything I've learned about life. It goes on.

~ Robert Frost

It is in learning through love that we set ourselves free. We all have life lessons to learn, and we can either learn them in a state of fear or a state of love. None of us get a pass at this.

Oftentimes, I am asked, "Why does this keep happening to me?" and I always respond by bringing up questions.

"Maybe you have not gotten the lesson. What is the lesson? What are you trying to control here?"

The miracle of being human is that we are exactly where we need to be. We are perfect and whole exactly as we are, and the answers to any of our questions dwell within us. When we turn to another person, even a spouse, for the answers or to fill our hearts' longing, it will inevitably lead to disaster. None of us knows really what is right for another human being.

I am not suggesting that we are not able to give one another joy and love; I am saying that we must act from our place of love, within us, and when we do, we no longer need the approval of others to make life right for us. Oftentimes, we get so caught up in trying to make another person love us that we are not tapped into what is really right for our souls and our evolution. We deny feelings and warning signs that the Divine within us tries to tell us.

Ask yourself what signs you are seeing. How are you interpreting events? You can walk through the doorway of possibility when your angels open it, or you can walk around feeling as though you are being pushed into the Grand Canyon.

If you are entering midlife, chances are you have been pushed into the Grand Canyon at least once. To illustrate, let's say you fall in love with someone and start to share a life together. Your spouse does not like something about you or your family, and instead of discussing it and working through it, you begin to alter pieces of your personality. You step outside your "truth." Even though you hear whispers, inside you, saying that you are perfect the way you are, you make the changes.

When you alter yourself to please others, however, you are not experiencing the world in a state of truth. You might grow angry at your partner and begin to pick at his or her flaws, demanding alterations. Perhaps he or she complies. After all, who wants to fight all the time? Soon, you are wondering why you and your partner are fighting still. Each of you has changed to try to suit the needs of the other.

You go on fighting for the relationship, thinking that if you keep changing to "stay" in love, things will work out. Yet, once again, the Divine within is questioning things. *This is not serving my highest purpose. How will I attract love from anger and fear?*

Still, you fight to hold on. You are dedicated to this relationship, even if it is serving no one and even if neither of you is being honest. Heck, you are married, and a monogamous relationship simply has to survive. Doesn't it?

Then one day, shockingly, you find out that your spouse has another lover. How could your spouse have done that to you? You, who were so committed to the relationship! How could the person who shared your home and perhaps children do this?

She/he tells you that the other person loves her/him for who they really are. He/she is leaving you, and you do not have a say. Just like that, your spouse is gone, and you feel devastated, wounded. Your reality is shattered. You can't believe this is happening to your family. You have just been shoved into what feels like the Grand Canyon.

Now, this story is fictional. However, each of us has had experiences similar to this one. If we look back, prior to the shove, there were signs warning us that the road was coming to an end and that we needed to switch course, but we did not.

The possibility before us now is how we look at our Grand Canyon experiences during marriage and divorce. We can choose to look back on our experiences with eyes wide open and be honest, and we can ponder the lessons taken from those falls. This may seem like the hardest thing to do, and yet it is freeing when we finally look at the situation from all perspectives, even those of our ex-spouses.

We are always making choices: the choice of how we look at a situation and the choice of how we act and what we say. This means we can change the story of our marriage and divorce right now. We can tell a tale of love and healing. It is all a matter of perspective and the desire to truly heal the wounds of the heart.

Sometimes, this is when a great group setting or a coach or therapist can come in handy. It is hard to change our own perspectives, especially when wounded and acting from fear. When we use the assistance of an outside, unbiased source, we can find new ways to look at the same situation.

It is vital to keep in mind that you are here to experience human manifestation for the Great Divine. You behold the world from your eyes, taste the world with your mouth, feel it with your hands and

11

skin, smell it with your nose. Each of us is unique and yet the same, connected always to the Source.

This is why, when we connect with another being through a loving interaction, we are lifted to a place of ecstasy. It is that ecstasy, even when it ends, that causes us to hang on to some of our relationships so desperately. In these sacred moments, we realize that it is in loving in this way that we are granted a greater ability to love all mankind. It is our ultimate lesson in intimate relationships.

When in a healthy, sacred relationship, we are filled with love, so we act from love and have a greater capacity to love all our sisters and brothers as well as all life on this planet. We can become miracle workers on Earth.

However, these relationships take many forms. I believe our soul mates are those souls that change our lives, teach us our greatest lessons, and assist us to grow in our ability to love in a deeper fashion. They are not always our lovers, and our soul mates are never responsible for our happiness. We are.

When a love relationship seems to be ending, we need not fear that there will be no more love. First of all, relationships never end. They just change form. Even when death intervenes, the relationship lives in our hearts. If it is God's will that we love one another as he loved us, why would he then keep from us the ability to love again? He wants us to love and be loved.

Some of the mythical aspects of love can keep you bound in hurtful situations, clutching to illusions. But if you honestly honor the love you shared with your ex-spouse, you create a breeding ground for more love to grow within your heart and the wounded heart of this planet. Love bears gifts that last a lifetime, even when a relationship does not.

When you continue to bear your story of divorce, you are doing a twofold injustice to yourself. You are not living in the present, which is your daily gift, and you are remaining mired in fear and pain. To help you break free, I offer you an opportunity to turn within and examine why you continue to perpetuate the negativity surrounding your divorce. Remember, we keep bringing into our lives that which we put out. When exiting a relationship, we need to keep in mind that we were born from love and we are born to love. Loving in the past never precludes us from loving in the moment. Love grows and feeds off LOVE.

You can reinvent your past relationship in a state of love if you find the gifts in the experience. That is how you will bring love into your life.

Love for yourself, your community, your GOD and your planet.

Dear Lord ~

I bless and release my ex-
spouse into your care ~

I am aware of the power of my words and
actions and ask for the divine guidance
to act in accordance to my highest good
and the good of all around me ~

I am exactly where I need to be
right now ~

Please make me who you would have me be
so that I may act
as you would have me act ~

Take from me my feelings of hurt,
judgment, anger and fear ~

I am at peace in your care ~

Amen . . . I'm in.

Week One

Questions and Divine Assignments

The unexamined life is not worth living.

~ Socrates

What is your divorce story?

Are you a victim or the villain? Are there shame and/or blame attached to the role you play?

When you repeat the story, how does it decrease your energy and deplete your joy?

How does telling your story serve you?

What are some simple steps you could take right now to change the way you see, and act on, your breakup and divorce?

Action: Decide whom you will discuss your divorce with, and let them know why you have chosen them (no more than two people). The people you choose should be those who will not feed into negative dialogue about your ex-spouse or the divorce, but offer support and a loving ear for your contemplation. Then create a list of people who, when you discuss your divorce, help keep you stuck in the role of victim or villain. Ask those people to gently remind you that you are no longer going to repeat this self-defeating conversation. If they won't stop bringing up your old divorce story, or if they allow you to continue bringing it up, ask yourself why. What are their motives for keeping you stuck in this story? Keep in mind that we can view these facts from fear or from love and that it is important to keep your judgments in check. Just notice and write your thoughts down. Be as short and concise as possible.

Chapter 2

Balancing the Scale
Of Our Emotions

Grief, Anger, Resentment, Fear,
Hope, Renewal, Courage, Love

Identifying Our Emotions,
Honoring Them and Moving Through Them

There is no place where the Presence of God is not,

*Only people who are not fully present
in the places where they are.*

You have only to be present to know all you need to know.

~ Ken Carey

The divorce is over, the battles have ended, and at last you are free to begin creating your new life.

But are you, really? Has the destruction of your psyche and heart ended?

For many of us, this is when we get stuck. Have no fear though. Being stuck at this point is like being in wet cement. It hasn't dried, and we can escape it. This is an opportunity to consider our true feelings, make peace with our emotions and begin to tend to our deep wounds.

When I went through my separation and divorce, I worked diligently with a therapist and coach to figure out why I made choices that did not serve me and why I had chosen paths that were self-destructive. My professional support team helped me build a foundation for an authentic life. When I was at last officially divorced, I became excited about the life before me, and I assumed my work was done.

It's funny how when the dust finally settled, I felt as though I were living in a ghost town and had to start the rebuilding process again. It was time to plant those trees and repair the old, empty buildings of my life. But something was holding me back.

What was this? I was no longer in love with my ex-spouse. I was excited about my future, and yet sadness permeated my being, and I was not sure how to shake it. In the evenings, when alone, I was faced with pain that at times brought me to my knees.

In the end, I knew that the only way to clear out the sadness was to shed some light on it. What I finally faced up to was my grief and regrets, a deep sadness over a life that was dead. I was forced to look at my own actions—even the ones that made me cringe with remorse.

I allowed myself time to meander in the rooms in my mind and body that were filled with the memories of people and places I cared for deeply but would no longer be part of my life. There were many people who had suffered because of my divorce and my actions, and at times my regrets, grief, shame and loneliness felt unshakable.

This was probably the darkest time during my divorce recovery but one that was critical for real healing and lasting change to occur. I intuitively knew that I had to sit in my feelings, however painful, and name them and honor where they were coming from. I needed to forgive myself and others for many hurtful actions AND then repeat as often as it took to process the depressive, dormant feelings.

Each time I did this difficult work and came through it, I realized I had a more compassionate heart for others who were suffering. The isolation, the anger and the grief opened my eyes and helped me see others from a place of love and understanding. I found that I could serve others in a more authentic way because I understood the pain they were experiencing.

It was during this dark night of the soul that I realized I wanted to empower others to find happiness and peace after divorce. So many people were and are divorcing, and I knew there had to be a reason why, besides unwillingness to commit. I pledged then to understand the reason and to share the gifts that come from releasing a broken relationship and reclaiming the one we have with our higher selves and God.

Holding on to anger is like grasping a hot coal with the intent of throwing it at someone else; you are the one who gets burned.

~ Buddha

Recognizing what you are feeling emotionally and physically is a critical element to the healing process. If you do not recognize your emotions, claim them, name them, feel them fully and finally work through them, you will not recognize them when they pop back up, giving old ghosts power over your future experiences and choices. You will mistake grief for anger and fear for safety. You will make choices based on emotions that have been encoded in your cells and will react to old experiences instead of your current ones.

Believe me when I tell you that these feelings do pop up again, and if you do not understand why and lovingly tend to them, the results can be disastrous and repetitive: something we will explore later in this workbook.

When we divorce, many aspects of our lives are like those of someone who experiences the physical death of a spouse. We are no longer living with a partner, there is no one to share daily joys with, our co-parent is gone, and our lover is gone. The financial landscape is completely altered, many social experiences are dramatically changed because we are no longer a couple, and we are faced to make decisions without assistance or support.

However, when someone's spouse dies, both sides of the family often form a strong support system, and in divorce, we often have to deal with anger from the ex-spouse's family, along with their judgments. When a marriage dies, we often face the loss of beloved family members because they must be loyal to our ex-spouses. The same is true of them. They lose the relationships they enjoyed with our friends and family members.

If we are parents, we must also deal with sharing our children, which can cause even deeper isolation, grief and loneliness. Being separated from our children and their lives is not a natural state of being, so the resistance to experiencing this is enormous. The related issues fill a whole other workbook.

Just thinking about the children can cause people to feel overly anxious, sad and angry. This is why many people choose to block out these issues and not feel their way through them at all. As a result, the emotional wounds stay present in their bodies long after the ending of their marriages and subsequent divorces.

I often see this in my coaching practice. The issues related to sharing time with the children can be tremendously upsetting, even when someone is working through it all with the support of a coach. Consequently, many people look for ways to avoid this pain. Many people fall into the comforting illusion that feeling better is more about moving forward into the next romantic partnership and less about falling in love with themselves and ultimately the world.

It is wise to direct your anger towards problems—not people; to focus your energies on answers—not excuses.

~ William Ward

One of the ways we self-soothe and avoid painful emotions is by running into a new romantic relationship, either while still in the bitter end of marriage or immediately thereafter. We have a desire to feel good and to be loved as we are. But the fact is, we must be in love with ourselves as we are before we can bring forth healthy, compatible partnerships, in which both people are free to grow and learn.

Here is a fictional scenario, based on years of coaching. As you read it, pay attention to the thoughts and feelings that come up for you. I call this type of action the Band-Aid syndrome:

After years of compromising who they really are, Bill and Jane have grown apart, and their marriage is headed for divorce. It is a "dis-eased" relationship, They disagree, fight, put each other down, focus on the negative about their lives and each other, complain about one another to other people and no longer offer love and support without some kind of conditions. Basically, their marriage has a kind of cancer, and as they feed the tumor with negative behavior, the cancer spreads to other areas of their lives, affecting their physical and emotional states, work, children and extended family.

Their spirits are in very fragile places. Then one of them meets someone new—someone who notices that Bill or Jane is great, beautiful, handsome, kind, funny . . . whatever. This new person doesn't know about the cancer in the marriage. An affair ensues. This new relationship helps the cheater forget the pain that surfaces on a daily basis.

What has taken place is the Band-Aid syndrome, and far too often this is the reason for the demise of a marriage. The cheater feels a boost to self-esteem, and through the new, utopian relationship, he or she is able to avoid the painful feelings surrounding the demise of the marriage. Discovering the affair allows the spouse of the cheater to complain about the situation and adopt a victim's mentality, which serves his or her ego.

However, even when a betrayal like this occurs, after an initial separation both spouses must deal with the end of the marriage, grieve for the losses, honor the emotions and heal the heart. Otherwise, they cannot move on from a love-centered place.

Affairs are one symptom of a dis-eased union that is no longer serving both parties. But it is not the cause of a marriage's end. I am not justifying or making excuses for people who break their vows and cheat on their spouses. This is not acceptable. What I am suggesting is that cheating is like a tumor metastasizing in the physical body. A tumor is a sign that the cancer is no longer contained and therefore much harder to treat. But the tumor is not the cause of the cancer.

Oftentimes, after someone has been cheated on, he or she assumes victim status, usually through the entire divorce proceedings and beyond. Victims pose with their anger and blame, and they enlist family and friends to support this coping strategy. The betrayal gives both spouses an out from the marriage, and neither of them has to process the real cause of the cancer within their relationship.

One day, though, the self-sabotaging actions used to avoid the real pain no longer work. Then, both of you are forced to deal with the only person in the room—yourself.

If you are going through hell, keep going.

~ Winston Churchill

In my eight-week program, which is the basis for this workbook, I would estimate that 80 percent of those that attend were cheated on at one point in their marriages. Almost 96 percent of the group members feel victimized at the first of the eight sessions.

However, most people who assume the role of victim, for cheating or other offenses, are focusing on the end of the relationship and not its entirety. Each partner needs to think about the actions she or he took during the marriage, along with the level of communication that was or was not taking place, and each person needs to review the contract created at the beginning of the relationship.

You must step out of your role in your divorce story before you can enter the realm of true feelings. You must see the demise of your marriage for what it really is. This is critical if you want true personal transformation.

You no longer need to feel powerless over the situation. You need to acknowledge how you feel, honor each raw emotion and place it in the correct room in your emotional house.

This is scary terrain to meander through, so it is fine if you take it one small step at a time, but keep this in mind while working on this chapter.

You are not powerless.

While exploring this territory, remember that powerful line from the Bible: "Though I walk through the valley of the shadow of death I will fear no evil. For thou art with me."

Let me stress that the key to this simple and profound statement is that you need to be ready to walk through the valley. You must fold up your tent and no longer be invested in staying in that dark, barren place where you were before.

You can clutch the past so tightly to your chest that is leaves your arms too full to embrace the present.

~ Jan Glidewell

Grieving in divorce is like grieving any great loss. Feelings about the death of your marriage will come up at different times during your life, sometimes invited and oftentimes not. When getting divorced, you are suffering the death of something that has been important to you. But you can choose to honor rather than suffer the bad emotions, and you will need to summon the courage to do this throughout your life.

I have witnessed healthy, functioning individuals grieve again for past marriages when one of their children is about to be married and they have to negotiate a wedding. It can also happen when exes are getting remarried and their lives are about to shift again.

Let me emphasize that no one gets a pain-free pass. Throughout the course of your life, you are likely to feel moments of sorrow and sadness over the end of your marriage and the many losses that occurred with it.

What I am urging you to do during this week is take an honest inventory of the places in your emotional body where you still feel pain, anger, grief, regret, shame or fear. Begin to examine why these feelings are there. How do they serve you now? You can't fix what you won't acknowledge; so if it scares you to do this alone, ask someone to work with you for the week.

A helpful way to recognize emotions is by paying attention to what our physical bodies tell us. Our physical bodies are so tapped into the Divine that they will not lie to us. We must also use intuition. How many times have we ignored intuition only to find out it was correct? Our intuition is a way of knowing more than we seem to know. This sense for the truth is our birthright as divine beings on this sacred planet.

Have you ever had a feeling of excitement over an opportunity your mind says is not right for you? Have you ever chosen to trust your mind over your intuition and ultimately regretted a missed opportunity? The excitement was your higher self, trying to get through to you.

The higher self is the part of all of us that is pure love, tapped into God at all times. Listen for it, urging us to choose from love and not fear.

Choosing from love always begins with loving yourself first. This is not a selfish act but a selfless one. If you care for yourself and love who you are, you allow others to do the same. You then have the ability to act from an interdependent place where you can love others for who they are not what they offer you.

How often have we ignored that intuitive voice and stayed in situations only because we were committed to them? When we act from that place, we are not being faithful to anything but the ego.

Another way to get in touch with your true feelings is by noticing the language you use that is self-sabotaging. When you are discussing your ex-spouse, your current situation or future, notice how many times you are saying, "yeah, but" or "never" or "always." These are words that keep you metaphorically stuck in a reality that is limited and painful. When you state to the world, "I will NEVER find another love again," or when you say, "I'll NEVER forgive my ex-spouse," you are using your words as tools of self-destruction.

Do you make statements such as, "I ALWAYS pick the wrong person" or "I am ALWAYS blamed for what took place in my marriage"? These declarations feed into the victim's mentality. Talking this way leaves you feeling helpless and unable to enjoy the present moment.

My favorite one is "yeah, but." Say it fast enough, aloud, and you will get my point. When you use these two words often, it is an outright refusal to accept the gifts that are before you. Yeah, BUT you insist on staying in the same place, even if it is not serving you or your relationships.

Then there is "I knew it was over BUT I was committed to the relationship." If it was over, how were you committed and what were you committed to? How was that making you feel?

I often hear, "Yeah, but how am I going to support myself?" Another line of self-defeating statements starts with "Yeah, but what will our children think?" The variations include "What will our neighbors think? What will our friends think?" Do you see how language keeps us trapped in negative emotions we are not even aware of or able to name?

This week, take time to notice the choices you make regarding your feelings. Do you ignore your feelings? Are they coming from a present-moment experience? Or are they old wounds in need of tending? It is time to heal the scars. Take this week to begin this process with love.

Dear Lord,

*My heart it aches and at times
I am unsure why ~*

*I consciously bless and release my
ex-spouse but need strength to
honor my own grief and loss now
that my marriage is over ~*

*Awaken the wisdom in me, so I might
rebuild my life from a place of love ~*

*Today, I use these feelings as tools for
growth and deeper understanding
of each being on Earth ~*

*I thank you, God, for this day
exactly as it has been given me ~*

Amen . . . I'm in.

Dear Lord,

*I bless and release all my
feelings into your care ~*

*I trust that through your grace they are
transformed
and I am healed ~*

*When I am afraid, I experience the emotion
knowing it is an illusion and I am
divinely cared for and protected ~*

*I choose words and actions
that feed the love in and around me ~*

I see situations clearly and from love ~

*This is a beautiful day,
filled with possibility,
and I am grateful ~*

Amen . . . I'm in.

Week Two

Questions and Divine Assignments

Seek not to change the world but choose to change your mind about the world. What you see reflects your thinking. And your thinking but reflects your choice of what you want to see.

~ A Course in Miracles

Have I truly accepted my life as it is right now in this present moment?

When I do, what do I feel?

How can sitting with these feelings and really experiencing them help me to process the death of my marriage?

Am I am holding on to fear and resentment from the past? Why? What would happen if I actively blessed and released these feelings to God?

Do I use negative language to describe my current life? How often?

Action: This week, notice how you feel when you discuss issues that resonate in your body (make you feel excited, happy, alive) and how you feel physically when you discuss issues that cause dissonance (feelings of worry, fear, doubt, anger). Which type of conversation or thought process do you spend more time in? Write down your answers. Do you find yourself watching negative TV? If so, this week commit to turning off programs that bring about negative emotions. Notice whether turning off negative programming leads to a change in attitude or perception.

Chapter 3

The One Relationship That Never Ends

Our Relationship with God

He said, "Go out and stand on the mountain before the LORD, for the LORD is about to pass by." Now there was a great wind, so strong that it was splitting mountains and breaking rocks into pieces before the LORD, but the LORD was not in the wind; after the wind an earthquake, but the LORD was not in the earthquake; and after the earthquake a fire, but the LORD was not in the fire; and after the fire a still small voice.

~ Kings 19:11-12 (kjv)

Now that you have spent some time in the rooms of your past, looked honestly at the part you played in your marriage and honored your ex-spouse, it is time to really start the healing process. This might seem like an enormous undertaking, but it really is not. All that you need for this dwells within the "knowing," found in each and every cell in your body. This is the essence of God, and there is not one living thing on this planet that does not possess this essence.

A Course in Miracles tells us, "Nothing real can be threatened. Nothing unreal exists. Herein lies the peace of God." This statement may not make complete sense at first, but humor me and read it over a few times.

Now, think back to your recent loss and change of circumstance. If nothing that is of God can be taken from us, then we have not really lost anything at all.

I imagine that some of you might be shaking your heads. But for the sake of your heart, just allow these powerful ideas to carry you for the next six weeks of this eight-week journey.

The kingdom of God is for all of us, and it dwells within each of us. Everything else is an illusion. When someone we love leaves this physical plane, it does not mean that his or her energy is gone. The energy has only shifted. When a partner we have shared our lives with leaves, it does not mean that our lives are over. It means, again, that the energy has shifted.

The love that we shared never leaves our psyche. We may mask it with fear, but the love always remains. God is that love, and it is this eternal wellspring of love that we can use to refresh our souls.

God does not discriminate, nor does God care whether you are married, widowed, gay, divorced, single, rich, poor or a member of a specific religious group. These labels were invented by people, and none of these categories have to do with your relationship with your God.

That is not to say that these concepts or categories are meaningless. If identifying with any of them fosters love and a sense of fellowship in your life, they hold value.

For instance, if belonging to a church helps you feel closer to God and your community and fills you with peace and happiness, it is a great tool for you.

The same applies to marriage. If the marriage inspires you to learn lessons and love deeper, and if it manifests love on this plane, then it is a sacred union. But if the marriage fosters anger, deceit, frustration, apathy and judgment, then how could it possibly be a tool for God? It can't.

It is for us to pray not for tasks equal to our powers, but to powers equal to our tasks, to go forward with a great desire forever beating at the door of our hearts as we travel toward our distant goal.

~ Helen Keller

Connecting to the higher power is the way to peace of mind and a sense of deep connection to all on this planet. This connection is the critical element to your healing process now and any time on your journey.

It's funny. When I first started to write this workbook, I left out this chapter about prayer because many people are put off by discussions about spirituality, and I wanted to write a book that was marketable and appealing to as many people as possible. Raising sales was not my aim. Rather, I was interested in helping as many wounded fellow travelers as possible.

For almost a year, I was stalled in my writing, until I had an "aha" moment and realized that the first thing I share when I teach or lecture is my deep connection to God and the absolute need for that relationship in my life. It was almost laughable that I was leaving out the main key to my inner peace.

For what? Fear!

Whenever I coach, I am asked what makes me feel alive, excited and purposeful, and to many of my clients' surprise, it is not my wonderful husband, great children or supportive family that I speak of first; it is the teachings of Jesus and my love for my Lord. Without that, I would have none of the other gifts in my life.

Now, my relationship to God is anything but mainstream, and I really do not care what God is to you. We are each unique, beautiful creatures, so I am going to assume that God may look very different to you. That is OK.

Actually, that is perfect. Let me explain why.

I love you when you bow in your mosque, kneel in your temple, pray in your church. For you and I are sons of one religion, and it is the spirit.

~ Kahil Gibran

I was brought up in a Catholic family, loving the rituals that the traditions offered. As a child, I was deeply spiritual and felt that my calling was to be of service to God. However, the only option for me as a female was to become a nun. I had a hard time with this, because I also wanted a family and wanted to give sermons, neither of which the nuns could do.

It seemed to me that my church had no real place for a young, modern woman, and this did not align with what I knew was the truth about Jesus. He did not discriminate, and he knew the value of both male and female leaders. I can actually remember praying to God when I was a little child. I heard answers back, and it was often a female voice doing the responding.

When I was eight, I had a beautiful vision of Jesus on Easter Sunday morning. Although I was young, I can still feel the sense of peace that came over me while staring at the apparition.

Afterward, I was so excited. I told my entire family, eliciting smiles from my siblings—"our little sister is going crazy" kind of smiles. My mother, on the other hand, believed me, and she encouraged me to build on what I saw. She said that I needed to trust and ask God for the reason for the vision, no matter how long it took.

I stay centered on religion and the Catholic Church until my world was shaken by the death of my brother Kevin. I was 15, and he was 24. Kevin was a strong, talented soul, and his life ended abruptly due to a heart aneurysm. Just like that.

How could my all-loving God just take my brother from all of us? What was the purpose of his having lived at all? How could God hurt my mother in this way? Well, I was not only angry with God, my faith in higher power was tested, and I began to question whether there was a God at all.

Although my faith was shattered, I kept attending Mass, due in large part to good old Catholic guilt. But I stayed involved on a very, very small scale. Eventually, I searched out other forms of spirituality and became very involved in the New Age movement in the late 1980s. I loved the idea of positive affirmations and of honoring the energy that abides in all things on this planet. The concept of karma aligned with my need for a just but loving God. I read books on Indian, Asian, Native American and pagan religious thought.

During that time of my life, I learned many new ideas and made some of my deepest friendships. I tried putting different genders and faces on the Divine. But my main discovery was that religious dogmas had little bearing on truth or the innate yearning in my soul.

The truth is that even when I turned my back on God, the Still Small Voice kept whispering in my ear, and God never turned his back on me. That, I now know, is not possible for God.

I was then and am now connected to that essence every moment of every day. I also discovered that God does not create the ills of this world; we do. Therefore, God is not responsible for making them better. We are.

It was during this time that I came to peace about the death of my brother and the many wonderful souls I had lost in my life. What I came to realize was that each of their lives was a gift in my life. Not I, nor anyone else, owned them, however, so I could not judge the length of their lives in a physical body as long or short, well lived or wasted.

My life was made richer by knowing my brother, but he was not mine to keep. God does not take from me anything that is mine.

Prayers go up and blessings come down.

~ Yiddish proverb

My spiritual quest showed me that spiritual truths transcend any human-made religious rules. I could read a book on Celtic spirituality and it would speak of the same principles in the Bible. I realized that the truth is the truth, and there is only one God, and that God is love. There might be millions of different human perspectives on this topic, but the truth is unchangeable, and God is unchangeable. It is really that simple.

We are all children of God, we are all connected, there are no justified resentments, and the only thing that is real on this planet is LOVE.

Please re-read the last sentence until you can repeat it with your eyes closed. It is this week's affirmation.

Can you imagine if this affirmation were the mantra on each person's lips each morning all over this world? How simple . . . yet radical! People would no longer be offended by different forms of worship, such as sacred art or music from traditions outside their own. Culturally, across the world, we would be free to express our connection to God as we chose without fear of judgment, punishment or even death.

It would not matter if you felt it important to attend Mass, go to temple, kneel in a mosque at sunrise and sunset or dance under the moon naked. It is all perfect, and in a truly tolerant society these differences would and should be celebrated. Each one of us is an individual expression of the Divine mind, and there is no one way to worship God and to express love.

God grant me the serenity

to accept the things I cannot change;

courage to change the things I can;

and wisdom to know the difference.

~ Reinhold Niebuhr

Wouldn't it be a wonderful thing if we could respect that there are different ways of living and worshipping? What if honoring Spirit is in fact what God had planned? I believe it is and that when we judge someone else's devotion or the way he or she lives life, we block our own light.

This leads me back to my childhood vision of Jesus and my mother, who told me to trust and allow the message to be heard on God's timing, not mine.

Well, it took 34 years, but I finally got it loud and clear. I heard a message that God has been whispering in many ears.

Jesus is no longer walking this Earth, and it is each of our destinies to experience Heaven on Earth for God in our own unique way. No other person can experience your life for God but you.

I was elated when I felt this truth in my physical body. I was able to let go of many of my judgments and fears. That is not to say that I have none and that I don't blow it now and again. But when I tune into my true nature, I can let fears and judgments go quickly.

Unfortunately, we often invest heavily in the things of this world, defining ourselves by what is outside rather than by what is inside. Focusing on the world and society and fearing both are the main reasons why the loss of a marriage can be so devastating. We so often feel that our value lies outside of ourselves and is based on what others think and feel about us, including ex-spouses. But my dear, sweet sisters and brothers, it is not.

Our true value is unchangeable, and it is based on God's love, which is infinite and never ending. We just need to deepen our connection with God and to create a viable relationship with our Lord. This can be done easily and even quickly through daily prayer.

The trouble with our praying is, we just do it as a means of last resort.

~ Will Rogers

Prayer is not about asking God for things. Prayer is conversing with God. It is how miracles take place. A miracle is a change in perspective, and when your mind, heart and being are filled with God . . . there is no room for anything else.

We need to look inward, and if what we find there is a loud, critical voice in our heads, we must call it out. That is the ego talking. Our ego is our mind separated from the truth, from God and from the all-knowing intelligence that links us together.

When we think with the ego, we consider ourselves separate and alone. We then make decisions based on fear and not from love. Fear of not having enough, fear that someone else might get more, fear that we are not good enough, fear that we are "too much," fear that we are somehow unlovable, and a list that could take up all the pages of this workbook.

Fear-based thoughts are illusions meant to keep us separated and stuck and in the dark. Remember, all we need to do is put our faith in the Still Small Voice, and it will lead us to that place of light where we feel tapped in and connected. Honoring our connectedness would end a whole lot of hate-filled energy swirling around this planet.

One of my favorite authors, Kathleen McGowan, wrote this in her wonderful book *The Source of Miracles:* "Every prayer for peace eradicates an impulse of war."

Every peaceful action takes away and washes clean an action of negativity. So the first course of action for healing this planet is not recycling some plastic but recycling your thoughts and consciously deciding to choose new ones. It is your first step to healing your broken heart as well . . . I promise.

My mom has always been someone whom I admire greatly. She has been a wonderful role model on many levels. As a mother, she taught me courage, unconditional love and the ability to heal with a kiss. As a woman, she taught me that beauty is about respect for yourself and how you see yourself. As a wife, she taught me the need for my own thoughts and passions outside my relationship with my husband. As a sister, she taught me how precious the gift of friendship was. And as a faith-filled person, she taught me the need for daily prayer.

Thank you, Mom. As a woman of deep faith, every morning my mother begins her day with God. When we were little, she would basically tell us to get lost, because she needed to have her morning meeting with God. At the time, I was irritated, but as I grew, I came to realize that it was during this time that she was able to hand her cares over to the Lord.

She and I have had many conversations about how she not only talks to God but listens as well. I have followed in her steps, and each morning I start my day by greeting my creator.

Because each of us is unique, I do not think there is one way to pray. You can pray while showering, dancing, driving, in quiet contemplation, shaving, walking, lying in your bed, making the bed, cooking dinner, getting dressed, doing your makeup or better yet while doing all of the above. I encourage each of you to start a daily dialogue with God.

If you are having a hard time doing this, don't get caught up in judging yourself. I know that, for many of you, your faith has been shaken to the core by your divorce. All that you believed your life to be is no longer, and you are trying to rebuild. Many of you are right at the foundation.

Now is the perfect time for developing your prayer practice. You are the builder, but God is the architect, and by communing daily with the planner, you will be guided to make decisions in alignment with your highest good. You will be using your spiritual mind instead of the ego, and I assure you that when you do this, it will lead you to places of which you could only dream.

During this time of rebuilding, don't rush into decisions. I say this not because you are not capable of doing so, but because it is better now to strengthen your powers of contemplation. Feel out any opportunity that presents itself. Is it something that you feel excited about? Pray to God. Ask God how this will serve him, and then finally stop and listen. You will get the answer.

In prayer, it is the quieting and stillness that we too often miss or bypass. We pray, we talk, we ask for this, we give thanks for that, but then, right when God is about to talk back, we are on to something else. We cut off the juicy dialogue that awaits us.

If we live by the Spirit, let us also be guided by the Spirit.

~ Galatians 5:25 (nrsv)

If you do not hear God's answers in prayer, consider the possibility that you are getting answers that your ego does not want you to hear. I know for myself that often I have heard the answer but thought, *No way! That is not right.* I then proceeded not to listen. I did my own thing, and when I looked back, I thought, *Hmm, I should have trusted my intuition.*

Intuition is God talking loud and clear. Do you remember the "Grand Canyon" moments of your life? Chances are, God did try to warn you prior to your reaching the cliff.

The hardest part of a prayer-filled life and yet the most rewarding is choosing to do God's will. Oftentimes, we think that doing God's will is going to prohibit us from living the life we want. It is not. When we do God's will, we have the opportunity to experience life on a richer, more connected plane.

I have always thought of God as an all-loving parent, sometimes paternal and other times maternal. Being a parent myself, I know that I want only the best for each of my wonderful children. Wouldn't God want that for us?

Isn't God capable of so much more than we could imagine? Just look around at this beautiful planet and the many amazing innovations that the human mind has created with the help of Spirit. By handing our lives to God, we are not giving up, we are surrendering, and that is a very big difference.

To surrender does not mean that you lie down and do nothing. You must remain willing to do your part to co-create the life you want. By surrendering, you simply allow the way to be shown to you. It is in surrendering that you find peace.

We don't have to figure it all out. By simply handing any issue to God, we free ourselves from self-inflicted pain. God cannot take from us that which we will not release to him. So let it go.

The old saying "Let go and let God" is a pearl of divine wisdom and a mantra I use daily.

One of the simplest prayers that I use every day is this:

It is my free will to do your will, dear God ⁓

Amen . . . I'm in.

Some other simple prayers are . . .

Today I ask that God walk before me ⁓

Christ walk beside me ⁓

And may the Holy Spirit that dwells within

guide my thoughts and actions today ⁓

Amen . . . I'm in.

and . . .

**I bless and release this (name
the situation or person)**

into your care, God ~

I pray for the best outcome for all of us ~

Amen . . . I'm in.

In prayer, you are surrendering your will to the Divine and stating to the universe that you trust that what is best for you will happen.

No fears. Doing God's will is simply following a path of love, and love is the only thing that is real.

You need faith to make your prayer practice meaningful, but I know that faith can seem elusive. Many of you are newly single, deeply wounded and feeling alone.

How can the third chapter and third week of this process possibly be calling on you to pray every day to God and to bless and release your ex-spouse and find your faith? Shouldn't that be for the last chapter? I mean, my God!

Exactly, my God.

Trust in the Lord with all your heart,

And lean not on your own understanding;

In all your ways acknowledge Him,

And He will direct your paths

~ Proverbs 3:5-6 (nkjv)

Without faith in God, it is hard to experience the healing your soul yearns for and knows as its birthright. Any healing will be superficial. You will make the same mistakes you have made in the past, and you will probably search for another workbook to help you figure it out.

We are not faithless beings. But we have faith in either what is within or faith in the outer realms of the world. It is faith in the outer world that has gotten most of us into trouble during our lives.

If we are divine beings, each possessing the essence of God, where should we be focusing our attention and placing our faith? On the inner landscape of our beings, that's where!

Faith in other people, faith in our physical looks to get us the part, faith in our education to get us the job, faith in a God outside of this planet or ourselves are sure ways to create a sense of separation and loneliness. It is time to place your faith in yourself and the God that dwells within and has never stopped loving you.

I have often heard the participants of the Flying Solo workshops tell me things like, "He/she completes me." I often hear, "I had such a wonderful life when I shared it with my spouse."

Many people say, "When I lost my spouse, I lost my identity." What I have always said in return is the core of this workbook and my most ardent prayer for each of you.

When you enter into another special relationship, I want it to enhance your life but not give you a life.

You will need to work on co-creating that life with none other than the ultimate partner, God, and I suggest you start today. You are the author, not the co-author, of the next chapter of your life, and with a little faith, a lot of prayer and some work, I know this next chapter is going to be your juiciest.

Prayer is the gift you can give yourself, no matter what state you are in physically, emotionally or financially. Finding that connection is the turning point to healing your wounded heart. It is my prayer that you will begin taking advantage of the most beautiful, fulfilling and intimate relationship offered on Earth—your relationship to God. Today, I urge you to begin your daily dialogue with God, and watch as the miracles unfold.

For Week Three's prayer, I humbly offer the Lord's Prayer.

Clearly, I am in love with Jesus and all he stood for and means to us. I believe his teachings transcend religious and political barriers, inclusive of men and women. It was a woman for whom he performed his first miracle, it was women who stood vigil at his death, and it was his beloved to whom he appeared after his resurrection. His disciples were men. His teachings were meant for all, then and now.

We have but one prayer that was authored by him, the Lord's Prayer, and I believe it is a perfect prayer, touching on every aspect of life. I encourage you to research it through books, essays, workshops, and of course prayer, finding your own meaning within the words. Your perspective is unique, beautiful and an expression of God.

In my opinion, the Lord's Prayer is the ultimate tool for transformation. I say it many times throughout the day and often reflect on the deeper layers of each word and its meaning.

Because there are several amazing books which have already been written on this subject, I see it as my job to merely introduce you to the prayer from a different vantage point and hopefully get you intrigued enough to learn more.

If you want to learn more, consider starting with two excellent books on the Lord's Prayer, both from different yet beautiful perspectives: *The Source of Miracles,* by Kathleen McGowan, and *Sermon on the Mount*, by Emmet Fox.

THE LORD'S PRAYER

Our Father, Who art in Heaven, hallowed be thy name ~

Express faith in a God that is parent to all of us, not some of us, a God who is love and holy.

Thy kingdom come, Thy will be done ~

Through prayer and our free will to do God's will, we will experience the kingdom of God.

On Earth as it is in Heaven ~

Through service to others and this planet we are capable of manifesting Heaven on Earth.

Give us this day our daily bread ~

With gratitude and thanksgiving we trust in God to provide us with all we need.

Forgive us our debts as we forgive those who are in debt to us ~

Through forgiveness all things are possible.

Lead us not into temptation but deliver us from evil ~

With faith in God, you are led on a path free of the sins that keep you separated from love and your highest good.

Week Three

Questions and Divine Assignments

Be still, and know that I am God.

~ Psalm 46:10 (kjv)

How do I describe God? What does God look and feel like?

Did my idea of God change after divorce? Did I feel abandoned? Why?

Do I have faith in myself or in things outside of myself?

Do I consider myself connected to each and every living thing on this planet?

What are my judgments and how do they keep me separated? Does this serve me?

If God is my parent, can I accept that he is a loving parent to every person, including my ex-spouse?

Action: This week take 10 minutes to sit and talk to God, even if you do not feel like it. Fake it till you make it. Does your mind wander? Where to? Are the thoughts positive or negative? Are they action-oriented? For instance, do you think of a to-do list? Notice your thoughts without judgment and then get back to conversing with God. Make sure that you are also listening. If you avoid doing this exercise, explore the reasons why. How is that serving you in the present moment?

Chapter 4

Forgiveness: The Ultimate Tool

Self-Transformation and Acquiring Peace of Mind

Then said Jesus, Father, forgive them; for they know not what they do. And they parted his raiment, and cast lots.

~ Luke 23:34 (kjv)

As we enter Week Four, it is my hope that you have begun a daily dialogue with God and have spent time considering the story of your past and the role you played in the dissolution of your marriage. I hope you have had some time to identify your buried emotions and work through them. More importantly, let's hope you have been nonjudgmental and able to do these activities from a place of self-love.

Now that we have weeded our gardens of yesterday's dead, overgrown plants and purchased seeds of hope from the Source, we are now given the tools to soften the hardened soil of our hearts. From this week forward, we will be tilling our gardens through the act of forgiveness.

For most of us, forgiveness is not a normal act. It's not something that we work on daily. Even when we consider ourselves forgiving people, we are usually pretty cheap when it comes to complete forgiveness. We may forgive people we love if they fill a need or love us back. But there are many other people we have not forgiven.

I believe most of us behave this way because we are acting from a state of fear. We have fear that if we forgive we condone behavior that does not resonate with us. However, forgiveness is not about condoning or even judging behavior. It is simply an act of releasing an emotion or thought that causes us pain.

Therefore, if you are offering your gift at the altar and there remember that your brother or sister has something against you, leave your gift there in front of the altar. First go and be reconciled to them; then come and offer your gift.

~ Matthew 5:23-24 (niv)

I do not know about you, but when someone forgives me of wrongdoing, it does not stop the gremlin in my mind from reminding me of how I blew it, or worse, from making me feel unlovable. That is because forgiveness sets the person doing the forgiving free. The wrongdoer has to find his or her own place of peace.

After divorce, there are usually many prisoners being held in our hearts—people we are unwilling to forgive. Our ex-spouses cheated and lied. They abused, manipulated and abandoned us; the list of what we hold against them goes on and on.

We may be angry with certain family members and friends, our lawyers and possibly our children. After all, our children often still love our exes, despite the hurt they have caused. We may be mad at ourselves and even at God.

If it is rational that when we forgive we release the pain inflicted on us by others or ourselves, why don't we do so as soon as possible? How might holding on to this pain serve us?

For many divorcés and divorcées, the pain is the one link that keeps us connected to our ex-spouses. By remaining angry and unforgiving, we feel entitled to talk about them and their wrongdoing, keeping them present in our minds and still a part of our lives. It also keeps us in the role of victim, and that pardons us from living our best lives. After all, victims are powerless over their own stories and circumstances.

Forgiveness is not an occasional act, it is an attitude.

~ Martin Luther King Jr.

I am often asked how we forgive people who have done unthinkable things to us or to people we love. I am asked how that sets us free. My answer is this: The act of forgiveness is cleansing. It is like tilling soil; it loosens the constricted parts of our heart, it eliminates what is no longer working, and it allows fertile space for new things to grow.

Adopting an attitude of forgiveness can seem especially difficult when we feel betrayed or abandoned. But the act of forgiveness can start with a simple prayer. Just think about the following words and what they might mean in your life:

Dear Lord,

Thank you
for the strength and courage
to forgive myself and others
with an honest, loving heart ~

I am free to move forward
in peace and with a servant's heart
to do your will ~

Amen . . . I'm in.

Being unforgiving is constricting. It cuts off life. Besides, who are any of us to judge others? I have yet to meet one person who is not in need of some forgiveness. In our humanness, we blow it every day, even if our intentions are the best.

I am not suggesting that you should not have healthy boundaries and expectations within relationships, whether they are with partners, children, family, co-workers or friends. I am merely suggesting that when someone hurts you, or you harm yourself or someone else, consider using forgiveness as a release from the pain and a way to attend to the hurt.

I like to call this "creating a white picket fence around the garden." Let's look at two fictional examples.

Example number one:

Liz's lifelong friend Maria has been late every time they have met in the past year, often canceling altogether. Whenever they spend time with one another, Liz feels that Maria is interested in discussing only herself. Maria oftentimes divulges information about her husband, who is dear friends with Liz's husband. This makes Liz feel uncomfortable. She feels that Maria has no concern for Liz's life or feelings.

Recently, Maria has developed a pattern of texting last minute and leaving Liz without a plan, often on the same day they have arrangements to do something together. Liz "knows" she is the better friend and begins discussing her resentments with their mutual friends. Many of them agree with Liz, and this temporarily soothes her pain, but in her heart she wonders why Maria does not make time for her.

Liz does not understand why Maria does not care about their friendship in the same way as Liz. Lately, whenever she sees Maria, Liz acts as though everything is OK, because that is what good, forgiving friends do. But all the while she is simmering about feeling disrespected and unloved.

Some time passes, and Liz notices that Maria has stopped calling her and rarely returns her calls. She feels even angrier. When she explains this to her other girlfriends, they of course see her point of view. She tells them that she keeps forgiving Maria, even though all she gets is less time and no return phone calls. Can you imagine?

Another year goes by, and Liz runs into Maria at a garden center, where she is with a woman Liz has never seen before. Maria is clearly excited to see Liz and gives her a warm hug before introducing her new friend. No longer able to mask how furious she's been, Liz says something snide and walks away from both Maria and her companion.

Before Liz has time to get into her car, Maria walks up alone and asks what her problem is. Liz, feeling justified in her resentment, lets her have it. She goes over the past events in great detail.

"I forgave you several times, but you kept repeating the same offenses!" Liz says.

When Liz is done lecturing, Maria looks stunned and tells her how she has been feeling. She informs Liz that her "perfect" marriage has fallen apart, and she has been unsure whether friends who are also friends with her husband accept the demise of the relationship. She attempted to discuss her marriage with Liz several times, but Liz seemed irritated and short in her responses. Because Liz holds conservative views on marriage, Maria assumed that Liz was not happy with her and Maria started feeling uncomfortable around Liz. She felt judged; so she looked for excuses to stay away.

After a while, Maria heard through the grapevine how Liz had been talking about her and decided that she would just pull away from the friendship. Maria believed that it would not be loving to confront Liz with petty gossip and risk a falling out.

Liz sits in dismay. She had not considered that perhaps Maria's desire to discuss her life was a quiet plea for support, nor had she considered that her moral viewpoints on marriage made her friend uncomfortable. She is embarrassed, as she knows she was arrogant to think she could be forgiving, judgmental and unloving at the same time. She sees clearly that these three do not work together. Liz also realizes that she was not the best of friends or even kind by never discussing her feelings with Maria. Instead, she talked about Maria behind her back.

The two sit in Liz's car and decide that their friendship is important to them both, but they need to make some "white picket boundaries" in order to feel safe.

Both recognize that Maria's career requires a lot of travel and that this makes getting together hard at times. Maria agrees to respect their appointments and not cancel last minute; she will think about the time and date before saying yes. Liz will be flexible about their get-togethers and shift them as needed. Both parties will be thoughtful in the process.

They both agree that they will work on speaking about their lives honestly and on not judging the other's actions. This means that Liz will have to be open-minded about Maria's very liberal politics and attitudes, and Maria will have to be tolerant of Liz's conservative viewpoints and lifestyle.

Tolerance is the keystone to renewing their friendship, one they both pray will work. They also agree that if they feel hurt or angry, they will discuss it with one another.

At the end of their conversation, the final agreement is that if either feels the friendship is not serving them or God, they will have the courage to bless and release it. Let it go.

When Liz drives off, she cannot believe how light her heart feels. Her resentments are gone. She has forgiven Maria and without even really working on it. She just opened her heart enough to see that harboring this pain was not serving her or Maria.

Liz feels unsure about their new relationship, as she knows she has to make changes and really listen to her friend, without judgment. She prays that she can do this . . . and she does. Years later, they are amazing friends. They have shared years of supportive, nurturing friendship, each providing perspective for the other.

Example number two:

Flo is angry, and she has every right. After all, she spent 26 years of her life being married to a man who was emotionally and at times physically abusive. She gave up her career and raised four children for Carl, and he left her for another woman.

How could this have happened to her? Carl could be cruel. He often put down her cooking and the way she dressed. He sometimes shoved her during arguments, and she always let that go. As a committed and forgiving person, she knew no one was perfect.

Flo had always commended herself because she never took Carl's crap. No way. She told him what he was doing wrong and that she would not tolerate it, in no uncertain terms. To have made so many compromises and then been left high and dry . . . she now feels bewildered, shocked, lonely and above all angry.

She had a lousy lawyer, and because of his inability to get her a proper settlement will have to return to work. She is pretty sure Carl's new flame is sitting pretty, and that makes her blood boil even more.

Flo is angry with God also. How could he have let this happen to them? In her search for acknowledgement, Flo decides to attend a support group at her local church. Thank God it is free. Carl is out on dates, eating filet mignon, and she is alone, heading to the back of a church on a freezing winter day to sit amongst strangers. Life is not fair!

During the first meeting of the group, Flo slowly begins to open up, although she has trouble digesting some of the material offered by the woman who is running the group. Too much love and light. Is this lady for real? She guesses that the group leader has had it easy.

It has been a particularly rough week, and Flo has been desperate to be out of her lonely apartment and free of the ache in her chest. As she sits in her chair, looking for a little encouragement, she is asked by the crazy blonde in the front of the room to talk to God and forgive Carl. Really, she has had enough of this fluff. This broad has another thing coming. She really does not get what Flo has been through; she is clueless. This is the last time Flo will be attending this class, for sure. She just has to get through it tonight.

Flo sits silently as others discuss their grievances, and one after another their stories give her the satisfaction that she is right and "Little Ms. Blondie" is w-r-o-n-g.

Flo cannot wait to give her a piece of her sage wisdom.

When it comes time for Flo to talk to Blondie during a small group session within the class, she lets it all hang out. She lets the gal have it, and, boy, does it feel good. She tells all about how she was betrayed, abused and embarrassed and is now financially in a hole. She does not have to nor will she EVER forgive the person who did this to her.

She asks Blondie who in her right mind would ever forgive someone like that, and she questions whether this woman can even relate. Feeling rather smug, she stares straight into Blondie's eyes and asks her what she thinks of that.

Hmm. The reply is in the form of a question, one Flo never expected. Blondie asks Flo if she would be willing to spend her entire life angry, racked with pain, and in unfulfilling relationships, feeling total disconnection. The second part of the group leader's reply drives the nail in even deeper.

"Flo, if you are unwilling to forgive yourself, you will only be cutting off the supply of love, joy and abundance that is there for you in this moment and each day forward. Forgiveness is the medicine needed for the wounded and weary soul."

Hearing this, Flo is flabbergasted. Did this woman not hear what she said? This is not about her; this is about Carl! She has been forgiving. But he wronged her, he left her, he abused her, he cheated on her, and he broke their family apart.

Flo lets the entire group know how she is feeling this time. She gets to her feet and proclaims her pain, only to be questioned again by Blondie.

"You say you were forgiving and loving, correct? Then why did you allow this person to behave in a way that was harmful to you, your children and ultimately himself? Flo, why did you stay in a relationship that was not serving your highest good? Why did you let this man hit you and talk poorly to you? Was this loving to you or to him? How is being forgiving allowing others to continue hurtful behavior toward themselves, others or our planet? It is not, Flo. You were a part of an unhealthy dynamic that stopped serving both. Why did you stay?"

Flo cannot believe her ears. She is being blamed for his bad behavior. She stands up to tell the entire group, "I stayed because of my children, because I was committed and because that is what good people do!"

Blondie calmly asks her to sit, which irritates her even more. Then the leader addresses the group.

"We stay in relationships that are not healthy for many reasons and then justify our actions. That does not make staying the correct choice for our higher selves or those around us. When we stay in a situation that we know is breaking down, we are there for selfish and self-sabotaging reasons, not for loving reasons. We stay because of our egos, not for our souls. We stay because the unanswered questions scare us. Where will we live? Who will ever love me? What will people think? How will I pay the bills? We tell ourselves that we don't want to end up alone. Most times we are not staying because we can shout from the mountaintops, 'Wow! This is my best friend. He supports my passions and my life's purpose. We laugh, we love, we argue, we communicate, and we forgive. This relationship resonates in my being.' Now, do we?"

Flo is bewildered. She never thought about why she stayed. She just stayed and justified the reasons. She recognizes that her true feeling is not anger but fear. She is petrified and has been for years. She also realizes that her unwillingness to forgive Carl is because if she does, he will be free to move on. What if he had a better life without her? What would that say about who she is?

She begins to cry. This is exactly what is happening, in her mind, anyway. Carl is out on dates; she is home alone. Carl is eating steak; she, mac and cheese. Is there truth to any of this? Who knows? Who cares? Flo is making this her reality, and she does not enjoy it at all.

Someone in the group asks Flo what would happen if she set Carl free, and Flo answers her simply, not thinking, "I would be free."

This is her "aha" moment, and the thought of being able to do something about her circumstances breathes new life into Flo's weary being. Over the next few weeks, Flo begins practicing forgiveness—note the word *practicing*.

It is not easy to let some of the old hurts dissolve. It takes hours of tilling to loosen some of the rock-hard soil, but at last she is free to experience new, collaborative relationships. She even has a say about making healthy boundaries around behaviors that made her uneasy.

She is excited about her life for the first time. She realizes that focusing on the bad deal she got in the divorce kept her stuck in the past instead of in the present. Now, she can take classes to increase her income earning potential and even pursue her love of teaching.

Flo works hard at forgiving Carl. Some of his behaviors still upset her, but she knows that she no longer has to argue with him about it. She is not his partner. She simply closes the gate on her white picket fence and notifies Carl that he is not allowed to come in when he behaves in ways that do not serve her self-esteem or his. She no longer spends her days guarding Carl's jail cell in her mind. She unlocks that door and leaves the building, spending her days creating her own beautiful garden.

The weak can never forgive. Forgiveness is an attribute of the strong.

~ Mahatma Gandhi

It is said that sin is anything that separates us from God and one another. Our unwillingness to release others as well as ourselves is one such sin. In order to forgive our ex-spouses, it is imperative that we honestly acknowledge the entire story.

What contract did we create with our ex-spouses that fostered the death of the relationship instead of the nourishment? This is a painful question, and this is why I asked you to spend some time getting in touch with your emotions, so that you could identify the feelings that come up.

Your ego's desire to be right often keeps you from being at peace or happy. How many times have you argued a point, felt 100 percent right and gone to bed with your back turned to your partner or not speaking to your child?

This is not to say that you should compromise core values. If someone abuses you physically, spiritually or emotionally, it is your responsibility to step away from the relationship. What I am saying is that people often wait long after divorce for the time to tell their exes, "I told you so." You can spend too much time in a state of limbo, unable to engage fully in your life.

What is it about the need to blame others that is so important? Looking for someone to blame is a driving factor in so many areas of our lives. We blame our politicians for the state of our affairs. We blame our parents for any childhood trauma. We blame society for not affording us the opportunities that we need to be successful. We blame police officers when we get a ticket for speeding. Some of us even blame our children for our sagging breasts and stretch marks.

There is a major aversion to taking personal responsibility, acknowledging when we have made a mistake and moving forward. My theory is that if we did this regularly we would become the luminous, on-fire, in-spirit beings God had in mind, and that would require a lot of work on our part. It would be fun, joy-filled work, but hard work. Perhaps that is why we put a bushel basket over our light and blame others for our inability to shine. It is our magnificence that frightens us, not our mediocrity.

When I have forgiven myself and remembered who I am, I will bless everyone and everything I see.

~ A Course in Miracles

When Jesus was being crucified, he asked God to forgive those who had harmed him. Can you imagine being his mother or a disciple? You have just witnessed the brutal torture of your teacher and loved one. Nails are in his hands and feet. He is bruised and hanging by flesh and bone from a wooden cross, suffocating, yet his final request to God is that forgiveness be given to his offenders.

Why? I think, perhaps, Jesus requested forgiveness to be set free of earthly limitations, and it was his final lesson to us, as spiritual beings having human experiences, that we cannot transcend a difficult situation until we surrender through forgiveness. There is no resurrection without forgiveness. When we refuse to forgive, we remain on the cross.

What about justice for our offenders? Shouldn't people pay for their wrongs? These are great questions, ones I urge you to discuss with others as you practice forgiveness in the days ahead.

Jesus did not say to God, "Forgive them, but let them die a brutal death." Forgiving others as well as yourself is surrendering to the concept that the creator of this amazing universe has a better way to make things right.

My personal philosophy for living a good life is this: What you give out, you get back threefold. It is the law of the universe. What you reap, you sow. So don't worry about another's justice. Focus on your actions and how they support you.

Offering forgiveness and being loving will come back to you threefold, in forgiveness and love, even if it takes a while to see the fruit of your work. However, being angry, judgmental and unforgiving will also come back to you. So what do you choose?

There are so many amazing stories about personal transformation through forgiveness. Below is a list of a few great books on the topic that I have found to be inspiring.

Left to Tell
By Immaculée Ilibagiza

If I Can Forgive, So Can You
By Denise Linn

Amish Grace, How Forgiveness Transcended Tragedy
By Donald B. Kraybill

The Shack
By William P. Young

Dear Lord,

Thank you
for the strength and courage
to forgive myself and others
with an honest, loving heart ~

I am free
to move forward
in peace
and with a servant's heart
to do your will ~

Amen . . . I'm in.

Dear Lord,

I am open and ready to receive
the miracle of forgiveness ~

I forgive myself and my ex-partner
for the wounds we inflicted upon each
other during our union and divorce ~

I ask that my mind and heart be healed
and the love we shared be honored
forever in my heart and mind ~

Through forgiveness, I open my heart to
the deep learning my soul yearns for ~

I thank you, God, for these lessons ~

Make me a vessel for your peace, love
and healing upon this planet ~

Amen . . . I'm in.

Week Four

Questions and Divine Assignments

He that cannot forgive others breaks the bridge over which he himself must pass if he would ever reach heaven, for everyone has need to be forgiven.

~ George Herbert

What is something you are not ready to forgive?

How does holding on to this resentment serve you now?

How does it make you feel physically?

Do you try to convince people to side with you against others? This can be happening at work, within your family, in relationships with your children or elsewhere.

How often do you judge others? Does it make you feel superior? Why?

What are you unwilling to forgive in yourself?

Can you honestly acknowledge your wrongdoings and ask through prayer for that person's or God's forgiveness?

Action: Write a list of people with whom you hold grievances. List them in order of the level of pain they make you feel. Pray for one person on this list each day using the prayer on the next page.

Dear Lord,

Today I bless and release _____
with love into your care.

*Please take from me any
resentment I am holding.*

I pray for _____*'s healing and
that* _____ *harms no one.*

Amen . . . I'm in.

Chapter 5

Examining What We Value

Who Are You?
Really . . .
How These Ideals Shape
Who You Are and
How You Relate to Others

Open your arms to change, but don't let go of your values.

~ The Dalai Lama

For the past few weeks, I have encouraged you to dig deep and stretch yourself. This week, I ask you to continue excavating. What is it that you cherish in this life? What principles do you value? You are about to plant seeds in your garden. The soil is ready, but what is it that you want to plant? What's next?

Values are ideas, actions and principles that have meaning in our lives. Many of us spent years in marriages in which we compromised our values without even being aware of it. In the spirit of compromise, we gave up core beliefs that were an integral part of who we were and are. As we start our new lives, we need to identify the principles and actions we compromised at the beginning of our relationships, during our marriages, and during the breakup and subsequent divorce periods.

You might be thinking, *Why? I have worked on forgiveness, come to grips with my feelings and really like having God in my life. Why should I name my values? I know what they are.*

Do you? How often do we sit and really consider what makes up the fiber of our beings? So often we think we know what it is we value, but if we put our beliefs in writing and discuss them, we realize otherwise.

We were told as children and young adults which values were "right," but not all of those ideals work for us any longer. What's more, our values are more than just moral principals. They are the things that we cherish and that make our hearts soar. Unfortunately, our values are too often compromised at the onset of a new relationship, during a marriage and even at the end.

Many of us say we were lied to and manipulated in our marriages. We say we value truth and fidelity. But have we always been honest? As a society, we do not value truth. We revise stories, we airbrush photographs, and we alter our physical selves. On dating sites, we list hobbies and interests that we would like to do, but we don't really do them. We even lie about our ages. If white lies are considered acceptable, what really is truth?

Let's go back to your marriage. In the beginning, during or even at the end of your marriage, did you falsely represent yourself to catch or keep the guy or girl?

You may have compromised to keep the peace: going to concerts even though you can't stand loud music; taking annual summer vacations at a lake, even though you do not enjoy the mountains, fishing and lake water and you love the ocean and the shore; going along with political views because you hate arguing and your spouse argues his/her perspective better; ending your connection to a church or temple your spouse doesn't like; converting religions, even though you don't really believe in the principles, just because his/her mom would have been upset if you had not married in the faith.

Then comes raising those kids. Ugh, the compromises that come with children. Do you see where I am going with this?

The value of honesty can be compromised under the guise of our being flexible and open, but our compromises often grow into something much bigger and more perverse. This is especially true when we do not even know we are doing it.

Freedom means you are unobstructed in living your life as you choose. Anything less is a form of slavery.

~ Wayne Dyer

What follows is an illustration of the slow and steady erosion of values and how it can eat away at a marriage:

Brenda and Max fell in love, and when I say, "fell," I mean hard. They were young, passionate and shared many interests.

When they first met, they were very much their own individuals, pursuing personal passions and interests. Max spent most of his Sundays in Central Park, writing poetry, drawing and painting. He enjoyed watching people interact and drew much of his inspiration from these experiences. Brenda had strong ties to her family. She drew great satisfaction from organizing memorable events for work, family and friends.

Brenda loved how strongly Max felt about human rights around the world, and his passion for the arts was inspiring. Through him, she hoped to do more for others and express herself creatively through music and art, all of which were new to her.

Max did not have a family that was close emotionally or in proximity, and he thoroughly enjoyed the silly banter at the dinner table at Brenda's parents' home. Max also admired her ability to complete tasks and stay on target, two things he struggled with in school as well as in work. If you wanted something accomplished, you need only ask Brenda once and the job was done.

They were both physically attracted to each other, and the sex initially was fantastic. Brenda planned many weekend getaways. They took long drives and spent hours discussing religion, politics and their futures. Both knew they wanted to marry and share their lives.

When they were engaged, Max wanted a quiet wedding with just immediate family and a few friends. He wanted to honeymoon at least two weeks in Europe. Brenda, on the other hand, wanted to include her extended family in the wedding and urged Max to allow her a large affair, which would also satisfy her parents.

Although she wanted to go to Europe, Brenda felt the money they received from the wedding should go toward a home. She thought it would be difficult to raise children in New York City, and she wanted them to start saving right away to get into a safe suburban neighborhood.

Max agreed to the large wedding and a week in the Caribbean because he loved Brenda and wanted her to have her dream wedding. This was when the compromises began.

After they moved from the city into a "perfect" neighborhood for raising kids, both chose to start a family. They often talked about the number of children they would have as well as what their kids would look like. They did not discuss how to make time for each other or how to continue to support their individual passions while raising their children. But they actually considered themselves better off than most couples because they spent time talking.

Their children were born, and Max got to work on building a career as a graphic designer. Brenda stayed at home with their children until they were in school. They made new friends through the children's activities, and on the surface everything looked picture perfect.

As the years went on, Max grew very dissatisfied with his work and longed to pursue his other passions and work against social injustice in the world. Brenda felt isolated most of the time and missed the long conversations she and Max used to have. The talking had stopped as the responsibilities of daily life took over. They took vacations but rarely alone, and when they did take time to be with each other, they would connect for a few days and then fall back into routines the moment they returned to regular life.

Then the earthquake happened, in Haiti and at home. Max could not believe the destruction in Haiti, and his soul screamed at him to do something.

He had two weeks of vacation time, which he usually used to go away with Brenda and the children. He decided to help out in Haiti instead, and he volunteered to join a church mission. Brenda was furious when Max told her what he was doing; she could not believe he did not consult her.

Max expressed his deep feelings of sadness and dissatisfaction with his current life, and Brenda said, "But this is real life."

She told him to reconsider taking the trip. "We can't be dreamers forever," she said. "You have your family to worry about."

Max knew in his heart that if he did not go, a part of him would be lost forever, and so he left at the risk of his marriage. In Haiti, the devastation astounded him. Max worked hard each day, and in the eves he would talk into the wee hours of the morning with members of his team. He felt alive and authentic again, and these feelings made him determined to make changes in his life back in the States.

While talking to a team member one evening, he was offered the opportunity to become the creative director for a nonprofit in NYC. The pay was less than what he was making, but the offer resonated in Max's being. The job involved spending at least three weeks annually in areas where the nonprofit was using its resources to make change. He felt exhilarated by this opportunity.

When he arrived home, he had so much to discuss with Brenda. He was on fire when describing his experiences. His children were excited for him and proud. When he told them about the job opportunity, his teenage children encouraged him to "just do it!" Brenda, on the other hand, could not believe what she was hearing.

Later that evening, Max and Brenda argued about the job offer. Brenda did not want to move from the house they had worked so hard to keep for the sake of their children. If he took this position, they would have to downsize, and she was not willing to do that.

Max did not care where they lived. He urged Brenda to use the time she now spent on the upkeep of their large house to pursue her dream of becoming a professional organizer. They could stay in the same area, in consideration of the children.

Brenda laughed at his suggestion that she start her own business and told him that he needed him to get his head out of the clouds. Afterward, Max sat up alone through the night. He decided Brenda was right. Who was he kidding? He had asked too much of Brenda. He told himself he would do a volunteer trip once a year and that would be enough. The next day, he declined the job offer and went on with his routine, miserable and disconnected from Brenda, but living the American dream.

Max no longer painted, he did not write music, and he felt as though his dreams were dying, but he assumed that this was part of being an adult. A year later, he went out for drinks with his Haiti volunteer team. They were preparing to head south again to offer their help. He found out that the position he had declined was available again. The gentlemen who had offered the job to him the first time urged him to reconsider.

Max did not discuss it with Brenda this time. He accepted the job. The next day, he went to New York City, looked for a cheap apartment, signed a six-month lease and went home to tell Brenda he was leaving her. She could not believe it. She was shocked and angry, but so was Max. He told her he understood her anger and was sorry, but he could not continue living in a relationship that was empty.

Brenda was furious. Empty? They had children, mutual friends, holidays, a home and lots of stuff. They shared memories. "Empty? That's ridiculous!" she exclaimed.

Max told her that they might have the outer trappings of a marriage but their marriage had died a long time ago. He found her stagnant and boring, and he was tired of being silent and feeling moody, which incensed her. Max and Brenda separated and ultimately divorced, and it is here that I suggest you fill in the blanks.

Courage is the most important of all the virtues, because without courage you can't practice any other virtue consistently. You can practice any virtue erratically, but nothing consistently without courage.

~ Maya Angelou

I have offered several fictional stories in this workbook because we can pull lessons from them. Did you see yourself anywhere in the story of Max and Brenda's relationship?

Do you see how making compromises about the things that define us can be an insidious disease?

We so often get lost in the trappings of marriage that we stop nurturing the relationship itself. We assume it will take care of itself; after all, we loved our spouses when we got married. Well, that is not good enough.

It will not be good enough in any future special relationship either. It is critical to understand ourselves and what makes us tick before we enter into any new, special relationship. This understanding is crucial before we make decisions about where we will live, what we will do for a living and what other relationships we will keep in our lives.

So often we choose careers for the money they will make us or because our parents wanted us to be this or that. We desire to live in particular towns or certain homes because other people will think we are successful and therefore worthy of love. Too often we do not make choices based on our values.

What if you hate to clean, you love to travel, you want only a small family and spending time together is very important? Why would you then choose a super large home with heavy upkeep?

Why be tied to a big mortgage and unable to take as many trips as you would like? Will you really take trips in 30 years, when the mortgage is paid off? What good is having so many rooms that your children almost never end up sitting in the same room?

Most of us are not in touch with who we are really and what makes us feel truly alive, but when we are, and have the courage to follow through, life becomes truly worth living and perhaps sharing with someone else.

You will read these lines a few times in this book:

You must be your own person before you can truly enter into a special relationship. All relationships should enhance the life you already have, not give you a life.

You can't get a life from someone else. That is an illusion. Two do not join to become one. When you are truly yourself, living authentically, you realize that you have always been part of the One.

Having your own life means you are using the sacred vehicle, yourself, to express and experience life for God. It is your job to live this life well and with purpose. Marriage and family might be aspects of your life, but they cannot be your life. When you honor yourself, you automatically give permission to others to do the same, and that is when the veil of separateness is lifted and you see that we are all individual expressions of one being.

Just as treasures are uncovered from the earth, so virtue appears from good deeds, and wisdom appears from a pure and peaceful mind. To walk safely through the maze of human life, one needs the light of wisdom and the guidance of virtue.

~ Buddha

Values are anything that we cherish and hold dear; they are guideposts on our journey through life. If we stop and consider if a decision or an action is aligned with our values, it will assist us in choosing well. So many times we ignore the red warning lights in our psyches and step head on into relationships and situations that don't serve us.

We too often deny the Still Small Voice within. We hear whispers that a reliable job is the wrong choice or that a scary, new venture is a wonderful opportunity, but we second-guess the voice and stop listening. Then, when we are stuck in the wet cement of our choices, we feel furious, sad, anxious and confused over how this could be happening. That is why it is so important to know how we feel, because our bodies respond to how our values are being affected by the circumstances of our lives and the world around us.

I am passionate about women's rights and personal freedom. The idea that human trafficking and slavery still exist, even in the United States and Europe, infuriates me. When I hear on the news that women and children are being raped and brutalized, I feel like screaming. Why? My core values are shaken by reports like this. The anger I feel is not good or bad, it is simply a feeling, but what I do with it is key to creating a purposeful, balanced life.

I can sit around and gripe with friends about the wrongs of this world, remaining bitter and unchanged, or I can get on my knees, pray to God, surrender to his will, and then get up, dust myself off and be of service. My feelings of anger and frustration are tools for transforming situations that I believe are unjust. I can use the beliefs and wisdom within me to make the changes I dream about in this world.

Here is a little secret we all know. We can't be effective at making any lasting changes in our lives or within any partnership or role if we are living according to someone else's set of values. We must, and I say must, know what we value in order to make choices aligned with our highest good.

These values are our guideposts, but life is ever changing. In this universe, nothing stays the same. Every minute of every day, the planet is in movement. The days pass from morning to evening and back to dawn's light. We are born, we grow, and we die and then are reborn like each season, day, hour and moment. The one thing that is changeless is our souls, and that is what binds us to one another. Our souls are pure love, and love is changeless.

No one is guaranteed that the things in life right now will be here tomorrow. In order to be reborn in this new chapter of your life, use your values as your guides and surrender to the changes. Consider who you are now, not who you were when you got married.

What are the things you cherish? What gets you excited? This week, spend time noticing how conversations, news, books, the weather and food make you feel. Your body is your ally. It will help you identify your values and understand what makes you tick. Love it, and thank it.

The next step is fleshing your values out. This is a very important step, because when you enter any relationship and begin discussing values, just using the words that name them is not good enough.

I use an exercise in my workshops in which I ask the group to name some of their values. I write the values on a board and ask who agrees with one or some of them. I have a participant explain the importance and definition of one of the values. Then I ask others to define that same value and what it is to them. You would be surprised how many times two people who share a value have completely different ideas of what it means.

For instance, I had one person say that honesty was the most important thing to her; she went on to describe it as always telling the truth about events in life. A gentleman in the class said honesty was important to him, but he felt it meant listening to his own heart and being honest with himself. He argued that each person could give an honest opinion about an event and it would not necessarily be the same as anyone else's. He wasn't concerned with whether others were being truthful; he felt he needed to be honest with himself.

Interesting, right? A full understanding of what you value and why is essential to defining your life's purpose as well as healthy communication.

You are halfway there, and I know you are beginning to feel good about the juicy, wondrous experiences that await you in this new chapter of your life. You are the author. How will this chapter look?

Let me list some things I value, so that you have an idea of the broad way in which I encourage you to use this term:

Life – I love being alive and feel grateful for the experience even when it is painful. I am excited by new opportunities and change.

Respect – Respect is a keystone of healthy relationships. It is respect for others and ourselves that allows us to leave relationships that do not serve us. Respect for other perspectives affords us the opportunity to grow and see things from a different vantage. Encouraging our children to respect themselves is a plea for them to love themselves and make decisions that support and feed that love. When we no longer respect certain people or things, it is an act of selfishness or self-sabotage to stay committed to them. It is not loving toward the other person or situation.

Time with people I love – Being with my friends and family feeds my soul. I get to share stories, laughter, tears and triumphs. Time spent with the people I cherish is like a juicy meal for my soul. When I step away from in-person contact for too long, I feel drained and depleted. What I have found, though, is there are some people I care for but must love from a distance in order to remain true to my highest self and loving toward them.

Mother Earth – I believe Earth is alive and that in killing Earth we are killing ourselves. Earth to me is the divine feminine, and she is sacred. From this value stems my desire to recycle, reduce waste, buy organic foods and create an indigenous garden. I know I could do more, but I honor what I am able to do. I find it hard to be around people who profit from Earth with no regard for her. But I work hard to recycle my feelings of frustration into things I can do to be a positive, Earth-friendly being.

My connection to God – This is my deepest core value, and when I ignore it, I operate from ego and feel disconnected. When I make choices without connecting to God, they are often in service of my big fat ego and end up unfolding disastrously. This core value ties to another: tolerance. Intolerance is the root of so much evil, separation and pain in this world. Just consider our religious wars. How do they serve God? They don't. They serve our intolerant egos. Because I know we are all one, I know the illusions we use to separate ourselves must eventually wash away in order for there to be true peace. World peace begins with our acceptance of one another's choices, as long as those choices stem from love of self and love of one another.

Dear Lord,

*My eternal self is changeless and
always connected to you ~*

*Open my eyes to what really defines
who I am that I might do as
you would have me do
and live as you would have me live ~*

*I give thanks for this blessed day
and every new moment
before me ~*

I dwell only in this present moment ~

Amen . . . I'm in.

Dear Lord,

I am blessed with my own
sacred blueprint ~

I know you do not make mistakes,
so I acknowledge and declare that I am
a sacred being with a right to be
here simply because I am ~

With you and through divine
connection to you
all things are possible ~

What I love and cherish is
right for me, and today
I will honor all the facets of who I am ~

Thank you, God ~

Amen . . . I'm in.

Week Five

Questions and Divine Assignments

Behavior is what a man does, not what he thinks, feels, or believes.

~ Emily Dickinson

Before we can answer this week's questions, we must first list our values and flesh some of them out. This week, we begin with an action: List at least 10 core values, define them, and describe why they are important to you. Discuss a few of your values with friends or a support group, if you have the chance, and ask them to describe some of their core values to you. It is useful to begin getting used to talking about what you value and cherish, so that you can easily identify when you are in sync with your highest self or making choices from the place of ego.

EGO = Edging God Out.

1.

2.

3.

4.

5.

6.

7.

8.

9.

10.

What values did you compromise in your relationship to your ex-spouse before you got married?

What values did you knowingly or unknowingly compromise when you were married? What about when you were going through your divorce?

How did these compromises affect your marriage or self?

What values will you never compromise again in future special relationships?

Beth Tiger

Name some new values you have acquired through the process of divorce.

Chapter 6

Finding Gratitude in Our Daily Lives

The Law of Attraction and Being of Service . . . Deliberately Creating Heaven on Earth by Our Thoughts and Actions

A human being is a part of the whole, called by us "universe,"
a part limited in time and space. He experiences himself,
his thoughts and feelings as something separated from
the rest—a kind of optical delusion of his consciousness.
This delusion is a kind of prison for us, restricting us to
our personal desires and to affection for a few persons
nearest to us. Our task must be to free ourselves from this
prison by widening our circle of compassion to embrace all
living creatures and the whole of nature in its beauty.

~ Albert Einstein

Ending a marriage can be a consuming process. We dive deep into ourselves, and the deep ache and pain can be almost unbearable at times. Endless issues arise, such as where we will live, who will pay for this or that, and when and for how long we will each have the children. Hard questions confront us. What do we say to the children? How will we spend the holidays? The list goes on and on.

After the divorce is final, many of our friends assume we are "good" and that all of the issues are resolved and we can just move on. However, there are new issues we have to deal with as we learn how to fly solo, and this is a time when stepping outside of ourselves and choosing to see the world with gratitude is especially important.

Asking God to show us how we can serve this world is the golden goose we are seeking. Many of us have heard about the law of attraction. We may recognize that it is right to have a servant's heart and be grateful. But how many of us are really integrating those concepts into our daily lives?

We reap what we sow. Remember seeing that phrase a few chapters ago? It is a paraphrase of a Bible verse, and truer words are hard to find. When we are stuck in our bitterness, refusing to work on forgiveness and focusing only on ourselves, we attract experiences that are isolating, frustrating, unfulfilling and self-sabotaging.

Before we go further, let's quickly review the last five weeks so you can see how the work you are doing is building up:

Week One – Lose the story, learn the lesson

In Week One, you were asked to review your divorce story and consider how staying stuck in the past leaves very little energy for the present. You were encouraged to notice how many times you told the story of your divorce, and you were asked to stop repeating self-sabotaging behaviors and thoughts that keep you in the role of victim.

Week Two – Identifying our emotions, honoring them and moving through them

Week Two was potentially an intense week. You were asked to acknowledge where your sadness, physical discomfort or anger were stemming from; you were asked to sit inside your feelings and figure out how to move through them. This was important because the challenges got harder in the weeks after, and if you did not fully understand your feelings then, the information that followed was going to fall flat.

Week Three – The one relationship that never ends . . . our relationship with God

This is my favorite week when I work with groups. It is the week where I usually begin to see the lights go on in the darkened rooms of the participants' hearts. How simple, yet exciting for people who feel terribly alone to consider that they are never alone and there is indeed a relationship that will last their lifetimes. In Week Three, you were asked to define what God is to you and how God works in your life. I made suggestions on how to deepen that connection through prayer and contemplation.

Week Four – Forgiveness . . . the ultimate tool!

Well, Week Four is often the hardest week, as forgiveness is difficult when we are still feeling raw and vulnerable. However, it is my prayer that you were able to see forgiveness as a powerful tool. Nothing works the same for releasing your past and standing in the present moment, excited for your future. Your Divine Assignment was to list people you held grievances for and to pray for one of them each day. If you are not still doing this exercise, start again today.

Week Five – Examining what you value

This was an exciting week, as it was the first week that I asked you to consider what's next. I asked what makes you truly unique and discussed the way your values define you. You studied fictional scenarios in which the characters compromised core values for the sake of love, which caused them to lose important pieces of who they were and why their spouses loved them in the first place.

You were asked to consider what values you compromised in your marriage and what values you would not compromise again in a special relationship. You were encouraged to start talking about your values so you could get comfortable naming them and sharing them.

All of these weeks were purposeful, meant to prepare you for Weeks Six, Seven and Eight. In the three amazing weeks that follow, you will explore the juicy possibilities of the life you are creating for yourself. You will consider what may be on the horizon, what your life's purpose and passions are, what you bring to a future special relationship and how to recognize a healthy one when it appears. Each week leading to this point will aid you in the weeks beyond, so refer back if you need to or stay on one week longer if you want to explore the principles a little further.

Prayer of Saint Francis of Assisi

Lord, make me an instrument of your peace.
Where there is hatred, let me sow love;
where there is injury, pardon;
where there is doubt, faith;
where there is despair, hope;
where there is darkness, light;
and where there is sadness, joy.

O Divine Master, grant that I may not so much seek
to be consoled as to console;
to be understood as to understand;
to be loved as to love.
For it is in giving that we receive;
it is in pardoning that we are pardoned;
and it is in dying that we are born to eternal life.

Amen

Each thought you think becomes something. It is not always manifested in the material world, but thoughts are like streams of energy, pulsating out into the atmosphere. If you focus only on your stuff, your life and your needs, you lose sight of the bigger picture and your life actually shrinks to fit. However, having a servant's heart and being grateful is an expansive state of being. Staying focused on God's will allows you to see more and be more.

Can you imagine what people must have thought when the Wright Brothers told them they were going to invent a machine that could transport people through the air? Can you even imagine what our forefathers would think if they were transported to modern-day America and experienced all the changes that have occurred since their time through the use of the human mind?

If thoughts become things, why limit what you dream about? Why get caught up in "shoulds" rather than listening to your heart and creating a life you feel excited about? Remember, we can either choose to think from a place of love or fear. You really can change your thoughts to feel better, do better, and be better.

Albert Einstein said it best: "You can't solve a problem with the same mind that created it."

A true revolution of values will soon cause us to question the fairness and justice of many of our past and present policies. On one hand, we are called to play the Good Samaritan on life's roadside, but that will be only an initial act. One day we must come to see that the whole Jericho Road must be transformed so that men and women will not be constantly beaten and robbed as they make their journey on life's highway.

True compassion is more than flinging a coin to a beggar. It comes to see that an edifice which produces beggars needs restructuring.

~ Martin Luther King Jr.

How you greet each new day? Are you waiting for someone or something else to make you feel loved, happy, excited or fulfilled? Well, if you are, you will keep attracting a whole lot of nothing. The universe is like a mirror. What you put into it, you get from it.

If you are being ugly, the universe will look ugly to you. If you ask the mirror, "What about me?" the universe replies, "What about me?" If you say, "I want this or that," the universe says, "I want this or that." But guess what the universe says when you say, "OK. How may I serve you?" The universe replies, "OK. How may I serve you?" The law of attraction and service go hand in hand.

Because you manifest what you dream of, the way to find satisfaction and peace with where you are at in this present moment is through a grateful heart. I do not just mean the obvious type of gratitude, such as, "I am grateful for my kids, my job and my health." These are very important things, but I would like you to stretch this week and find true plentitude in your present state. Think of the many things you are grateful for and start writing them down every day. This exercise will only take a few minutes, less than five, but it is essential.

We attract that which we think, so if we think with a grateful heart, we attract more positive experiences. We are also able to recognize lessons faster when an experience seems painful or challenging. We can choose to change our minds and find things to be grateful for, even within hard circumstances.

Finding satisfaction in the present gives peace of mind. So today, begin looking around for simple things that make your daily life fun and filled with joy. What gives your life greater meaning? Tonight, right before bed, write down what you are grateful for; include the biggies, but don't stop there. By doing this before bed, you are taking your focus off any stress and putting your mind into a better state prior to the healing that happens while you slumber.

P.S. Each night, try coming up with at least five new things for which you are grateful. I will give you a few simple examples to get the ideas flowing, just in case you feel stumped.

Too often we underestimate the power of a touch, a smile, a kind word, a listening ear, an honest compliment, or the smallest act of caring, all of which have the potential to turn a life around.

~ Leo Buscaglia

Over 16 years ago, I started a silly tradition amongst my closest friends. My very dear friend Susan was having a really rough time. Her business was very slow, and she was in terrible pain. She was later diagnosed with rheumatoid arthritis. Her days were difficult to get through. At the time, we were sharing a studio apartment with our two dogs, and watching her struggle to get out of bed and then go through 8- to 14-hour days on her feet at her store was painful for me to witness.

One afternoon, I was walking through a department store and noticed the most ridiculous pair of socks. They made me giggle, and a thought came to me. *I should get those for both of us, so when we look down, we are reminded not to take ourselves so seriously. Besides, if they make me laugh, I am sure they will make Susan laugh too.*

At the time they were an expense I really could not afford. They were $16 a pair! But I bought them anyway and sped over to her store to give them to her. I walked in and found her almost in tears. She was tallying the day's sales, which were not enough to pay the bills, and her hands were red and swollen. I told her to sit down, and I began tallying the cash drawer for her. While she was sitting there, her head in her hands, I told her I had purchased her a present, and immediately her face lit up. I gave her the bag, and when she opened it, she started to laugh hard. We both started laughing and, like two little kids, ripped off our shoes and boring socks and put on our very first pair of "happy socks."

Both Susan and I still have that first pair of happy socks, and through the years we have invited more people into the happy sock family. Whenever I am going to speak to a large group and am not wearing high heels or sandals, I wear ridiculous socks. It is a reminder to me to not take it all so seriously. When I travel, I do not buy my children T-shirts or useless souvenirs. I purchase happy socks. We all need to wear socks, right? My happy socks are something I am grateful for every time I wear them or give them as a gift. Bet you want to go get a pair for yourself now.

At times our own light goes out and is rekindled by a spark from another person. Each of us has cause to think with deep gratitude of those who have lighted the flame within us.

~ Albert Schweitzer

Another small thing that I have been so grateful for is Aromatherapy. Back in the early '90s, I was a practicing massage therapist. I was formally trained in the art of Aromatherapy, which was a very new science in the States. I loved working with these living energies from the natural world and realized I could create better health through these gifts from nature.

During my divorce, I had very little money and lived in a tiny little cottage. My home always smelled wonderful though, and when I was feeling low, I knew that if I diffused a little orange and lemon, my spirits would be lifted. Friends would come over and tell me how special my little cottage was. I am sure the effects the oils had on them was a large part of their reaction.

No matter where I have lived, I have always been able to create a little heaven with these allies. As I write this, I look over at my diffuser filled with frankincense and rosewood and feel so grateful for the simple gift of my sense of smell. It connects me to the natural world and inspires me as well.

Yet another example of a little thing making a huge difference is the gal at my local coffee shop. No matter what mood I am in, when I walk in, before I even get to the front of the line, she has my coffee prepared just the way I like it and always greets me with a smile.

How fantastic. What a gift. It makes me feel noticed and honored. I have many times been instantly transformed by her grace and positive energy and wonder if she realizes what a difference she is making in other peoples' lives by simply putting love into each action she performs at work.

I am also reminded how blessed I am that I live in a country where I can go safely and get a cup of coffee. In this one example, there are a myriad of things for which I am grateful.

Gratitude is riches. Complaint is poverty.

~ Doris Day

Today, dear God, it is my will to do your will.

When I wake up each morning, this is the line that I say, and many days I feel as though I accomplish that. On other days, I do not. When that happens, I work on forgiving myself and knowing that the next day I get to begin again.

When I begin my day surrendering the plan to God, I am often surprised at the amazing gifts I receive throughout the day. I look back over the last nine years and can say that whenever I have surrendered what I was holding on to tightly and just allowed God to work through me, the outcome has always, and I mean always, been better than I could have imagined.

When I got divorced, I returned to massage therapy. After years of running a construction company with my ex-husband, I had no other skills to fall back on, and I needed a flexible job, as my youngest child was two. My practice grew slowly, but it grew. I looked at bodywork as an act of service not only the receiver but for myself as well. I enjoyed the flexible hours and felt as though I was doing God's work, helping people to feel better in their bodies.

After a few years though, I began to feel tired of the work. Really, this path had run its course, and I had no interest in doing massage anymore. I had become a bitter giver, and each massage I did felt like a chore. I was just doing it to receive the payment; no longer was I giving from a servant's heart. Not surprisingly, my practice began to decrease, and I soon found a cyst on my wrist.

I knew intuitively that I was sabotaging myself, but I marched right into my fiancé's office and asked him, "Now, what am I supposed to do? I have a cyst on my wrist and was told I should not do massage, and I don't want to do it anyway!"

He calmly looked at me and asked me what was it that I loved about doing the bodywork. I sat and really thought about it and then replied, "I love empowering people; I love talking with my clients and making them feel connected to something greater than themselves. I love being a conduit to help others on their path, and I love watching people awaken to their potential well-being."

Thank God for that man—although, that is chapter eight; more about that later. After talking to him I realized that I did not dislike bodywork as much as I felt disconnected from why I was doing the work in the first place. Most of my clients wanted just a 50-minute rubdown and did not want to collaborate on their health or well-being. They expected to come to me and for me to make them feel better.

Hmm. I knew I was onto something, but I wasn't sure what it was. I did not enjoy my career anymore and was unsure what next step to take. I was exhausted. I still had my children to care for and a mortgage to pay, but I also knew I wanted to be of service to others and this world.

I felt pushed to consider how my work might do that, but I was unsure where to begin.

Each night I wrote in my gratitude journal, and each morning I prayed that the answers would be awakened in me. I stopped trying to find a career and instead went about my days considering what my strengths were, and that is when God opened a door and showed me a new path. Coaching.

At first I questioned myself and this path. How could I do this? Where would I get clients? How would I pay for it? What if I failed at it? Whenever I began fear-based thinking, my life stopped flowing; I could actually feel it choking up. Every time I thought of all the possibilities in a positive way, it would resonate; I was excited and felt clear and filled with hope.

I did my research, chose what I considered to be one of the best programs, emptied out my IRA and took a leap of faith. The study was amazing. I felt right on target and could not believe how blessed I felt while working on becoming a coach. I became certified in early 2006 and began my practice shortly thereafter. It was slow going at first, but by surrendering and offering my work to God, I was given little signposts that have led me to this point.

A man is a method, a progressive arrangement; a selecting principle, gathering his like to him, wherever he goes.

~ Ralph Waldo Emerson

I do not walk around wearing rose-colored glasses. My life has not been always easy, and at times it has downright sucked! I just know for sure that I can choose to be grateful for the experience, try to learn from it and allow God to work through me so that I can be an agent for positive change. So can you.

When we serve others, we are serving ourselves, and when we withhold our love from others, we are withholding from ourselves. It's that simple. So this week, I challenge you to consider how and where you can be of service, changing this world and your life, and I would like you to view service as many things, not as just the obvious ways we are of service to one another.

Consider the things that anger you, and think about how you might use your passion for change. Consider the things you are excellent at. Can you share these talents with others?

Consider your prayer life. When you pray for peace or for someone who has caused you harm, you are sending out energy that negates negativity. So the simple act of prayer is service.

Consider your resources. If you have abundance, let some of it go, and see what dividends you receive in return.

Consider your pain. If you have come through the valley of the shadow of death, can you offer a hand to help someone else come through it?

Doing these things in tandem will bring you the greatest fulfillment you can imagine. It is like water for your garden.

In lieu of a traditional prayer, I decided a quote from Gandhi is more fitting for this week. Cut it out; paste it to your mirror; repeat daily.

Keep your thoughts positive,
Because your thoughts become your words.

Keep your words positive,
Because your words become
your behaviors.

Keep your behaviors positive,
Because your behaviors
become your habits.

Keep your habits positive
Because your habits become your values.

Keep your values positive,
Because your values become your destiny.

~ Gandhi

Week Six

Questions and Divine Assignments

A person will sometimes devote all his life to the development of one part of his body—the wishbone.

~ Robert Frost

What am I grateful for right this moment? List as many things as you can in one minute.

Do I look at the world with a grateful heart or a heart of longing and dissatisfaction?

Am I mindful and living in this present moment or stuck in the past or future?

How have my thoughts created experiences I did not want in my life?

What can I do to "change" my mind and begin thinking from a place of love and gratitude?

What are ways I can be of service today?

Action: This week, make a pledge to God to be of service each day. At the end of the week, decide how you can use your talents to serve others, pray on it and then commit to take action. Write your plan down, and ask someone to hold you accountable for getting the action done.

Chapter 7

Love in All Its Forms

And the Romantic Relationship

One of the teachers of the law came and heard them debating. Noticing that Jesus had given them a good answer, he asked him, "Of all the commandments, which is the most important?"

"The most important one," answered Jesus, "is this: 'Hear, O Israel: The Lord our God, the Lord is one. Love the Lord your god with all your heart and with all your soul and with all your might and with all your strength.' The second is this: 'Love your neighbor as yourself.' There is no commandment greater than those."

~ Mark 12:28-31 (niv)

When the dust settles after divorce and we consider what is next, some of us have an overwhelming desire to find the next partner. We obsess about finding someone who will complete us, finally. Before doing an inventory or figuring out who we are or what we want, we forge ahead, registering on every dating site and asking every friend to introduce us to potential mates. We are petrified we will be alone forever, so we feel as though must find our next husband or wife. Now.

The anger and fear gremlins talk many others of us into doing nothing. We nurse the notion that we are so wounded from that last disaster that it is wise to avoid new relationships. We do not want to go through the hassle of putting ourselves out there. After all, what if we did meet someone? Jeez. We look at our history and see that we are clearly not good judges of character, so it is best to just be alone. It's safe.

Whatever you're feeling as you begin this chapter, I am going to ask you to read the next few pages with an open mind and let go of some of your preconceived notions about romance and marriage. At the end of this chapter, I will offer some re-entry dating tips. You can take what feels like truth to you and leave the rest behind. I share my perspective and experience only as aids. If some ideas fall flat and do not speak to you, that's OK. At this point in this book, I am confident that you are tapped into your personal truth and are beginning to look at your life through the eyes of love, more than viewing it from fear.

To love oneself is the beginning of a lifelong romance.

~ Oscar Wilde

What is love really?

Even in the ancient world, people thought that love took many forms, and they gave it different names. In Greece, there was a word for romantic love–*eros*. There was *agape*, a word for the way God loves us. *Philia* was a word for love between siblings or friends. There were several other Greek names used to describe love in its various guises, but the point I want to make is that love takes many forms, and the feelings of love are different within each relationship we experience.

To say you want to be in love is kind of odd, really. Chances are, you already are in love. If you have children, you are in love; if you have friendships, you are in love; if you have a pet, you are in love; and if you feel excited about your work and service, you are in love.

In our modern culture, we put so much emphasis on romantic love that when it is gone from our lives, we live in a delusion that we are alone and do not have love in our lives. It is often from this twisted perception that we make decisions about needing a romantic relationship or avoiding one altogether.

For this week and beyond, I am going to suggest that instead of looking for love outside yourself, you nurture the love affair that you will always have access to, the relationship between yourself and God.

If we do not enjoy our own company, we will never be satisfied with other relationships, because we will look to them to feed something in us that they cannot.

Love and compassion are necessities, not luxuries. Without them humanity cannot survive.

~ The Dalai Lama

A deluded feeling of starvation causes us to seek the love of another. It is from this self-sabotaging place that we act in many relationships and ultimately become dissatisfied within them.

No other person on this planet can be everything to someone else. Only you can do that for you.

We are often so focused on finding someone or something outside of ourselves to give us peace, deep satisfaction and love that we miss the point of our very existence. We are here to create heaven on Earth. We are not here by accident.

We are here as unique, individual expressions of God's love, and we already have the unconditional love we yearn for, as we are all God's beloved children. So you see, the romantic relationship is merely one expression of God's love in this world. Just one.

At this moment you are already connected through God's love to each person on this planet and to the Source. So the first step in being open to any future relationship is to stop putting limits on the miracles and experiences God has in store for you. Surrender, and work on loving yourself and your experience in this very moment.

Are you working from a grounded place? You must feel complete to tend the sacred garden with a beloved.

People who enter your experience should enhance your life, but they should not seem to give you one. If they do, you will once again find yourself playing a supporting role in someone else's story. You have to stop looking and start living in order to receive God's gifts, including romantic relationships.

Let us more and more insist on raising funds of love, of kindness, of understanding, of peace. Money will come if we seek first the Kingdom of God. The rest will be given.

~ Mother Teresa

When I first was divorced, I was too petrified to enter into a new relationship. I used to say that I would never get remarried. After all, I knew the poor choices I had made in the past. I had come to believe that most people were dishonest with themselves and one another and could not commit to anything.

Wow. Can you imagine what I was attracting in the beginning? Those thoughts were affirmed in the situations I attracted, and it wasn't until after some fantastic coaching and therapy that I considered what my life might look like if I stopped declaring what was or was not in my future.

After a while, learning to fly solo became extremely exciting for me. I realized that I was still holding on to my ex-spouse with threads of judgment and anger, and I began working with the principles I have shared in this book.

On one sunny Sunday afternoon, sitting alone on my front porch, admiring my little garden and feeling so content with just myself, I came up with a novel idea. I would start blessing my past marriage for gifts I had in the present moment.

At first all I came up with was my two beautiful children. I poured a glass of wine, turned on some Joni Mitchell and just sat and appreciated my past. I was looking for the hidden gems, and I could not believe how easy I could list them once I asked for guidance.

- The little cottage I was living in. Although I held a mortgage, it was the first house we purchased together, and it was all mine.

125

- My ability to manage money. Prior to getting married, I was a disaster at managing a checkbook and always had debt. Now, I was debt free, except my mortgage, and I ran my household budget efficiently. I was unafraid to take healthy risks when necessary.

- Creating savings. My ex was a diligent saver. I was not. I learned that putting even a little bit away added up quickly.

- Running a small business effectively. Through trial and error, working alongside my ex-husband, I learned organizational skills to run a small business. This was something that was really coming in handy for my own massage practice.

- Reclaiming my identity. Through losing my sense of self in my marriage, something I blame no one for, and through sinking to depression and self-loathing at the end of my marriage, I was forced to either reclaim my life or wither. I looked around that afternoon, as the sun was beginning to set, and I realized that the largest blessing of my failed marriage was the pain I went through at the end. I wanted more than ever to fulfill my life's promise, and I knew I would not have these new perspectives or the compassion I now felt for others had I not traveled through my own personal hell.

I call this list, and several other subsequent lists I have compiled, my wedding gifts. This week, you are asked to consider what your wedding gifts are.

All discarded lovers should be given a second chance, but with somebody else.

~ Mae West

When we bless our pasts, we carry forward the love we had and honor what was good. We automatically give our hearts space for new relationships in all forms.

About five years ago, my current husband, Tim, described how love grows. He was talking to my daughter about his love for her as his stepdaughter. She asked her stepdad if he could love her as much as his children. When he said that he already did, rather matter-of-factly, she replied, "Well, how? Where does the love come from? Do you have to divide it up?"

Tim told her that when his first child was born, a son, he wondered how he could ever love another as much as he loved his precious baby boy. When his ex-wife was pregnant a second time, he was afraid that he would have to divide his love and couldn't imagine doing that. His daughter was born, and as he held his new daughter he could not believe it. He just loved more. His love for his son had not divided; it had multiplied.

He told my daughter that loving creates more love. Being the sage little being that she was, she replied, "Kinda like the Grinch, right? His heart grew?" Tim and I cracked up and told her she was spot on and that now that we were married there was just more love.

We have explained to our kids that they do not have to divide their love for their mom or their dad in order to love their stepmom and stepdad. They are allowed to have more people to love.

I know that love grows from love. You can't hold on to hate and anger for your ex-spouse or any past relationship, including those you have or had with your parents, and expect to attract love into your lives. Hate, shame, anger and blame build huge walls that keep the love out.

Beth Tiger

Oftentimes, the one thing we are trying to avoid, being alone, is the one thing we create by our unjustified resentments. I am not talking about being physically alone; I am speaking about loneliness. Being alone is not bad in and of itself.

As I write this, I have been alone with just my Great Dane for company for the past four days, and although I love my family, these four days have been such a gift. I have enjoyed this time with just God and the dog immensely. I needed time alone to recharge and reconnect. We yearn for connection, and yet many times our actions and choices lead us further from deep, meaningful connection.

There is more to sex appeal than just measurements. I don't need a bedroom to prove my womanliness. I can convey just as much sex appeal, picking apples off a tree or standing in the rain.

~ Audrey Hepburn

After my divorce, I became truly content with my life as it was. The idea of meeting or not meeting a future partner was something I did not even think about. I was having fun and enjoying new friendships.

I was challenging myself to do things that scared me, such as getting my motorcycle license and going to a movie all by myself. I was tending a garden, reconnecting with my family, and relishing my time with my two beautiful children. I was in my present moment, open to whatever God had planned and loving every minute of it. By stretching myself emotionally, physically and socially, I made some of the deepest and lasting friendships I have today.

At one point, I decided that as a service offering for all the blessings I felt, I would participate in the AVON walk for breast cancer in New York City. I spent months caring for my body, training for the walk and raising money for this beautiful cause.

The walk itself was an awe-inspiring three days. We walked with survivors as well as people struggling with the disease. The overwhelming feeling of gratitude I had during these three days was transformative. I was buzzing with life, and after I finished, I called one of my dear friends and asked if she would go out with me. I wanted to celebrate my walk into the next chapter of my life.

Unshowered and dressed in jeans and cowboy boots, I went to meet her and some other friends at a biker bar, a place where my brother would meet up with friends after riding dirt bikes, and that's when I walked into my current husband. Of course, right? The point of telling this story in this chapter is that it was when I was not looking outside of myself for fulfillment that God plopped my beloved in front of me.

The lesson of all of this is simple yet so hard to really put into action. Stop looking, stop avoiding, and start living your life exactly as it is right now. Detach from the outcome and open yourself up to whatever God has planned for you. If God has another romantic relationship planned, you will recognize it as the beautiful gift it is: not something you cling to, but something you cherish and nurture each day it is in your life.

My beloved spake, and said onto me,

Rise up, my love, my fair one, and come away.

For, lo, the winter is past;

The rain is over and gone;

The flowers appear on the earth;

The time of the singing is come,

And the voice of the turtle-dove is heard in our land;

The fig-tree ripenth her green figs,

And the vines are in blossom;

They give forth their fragrance.

Arise, my love, my fair one, and come away.

~ Song of Solomon 2:10-13 (asv)

What is a romantic relationship? It is a garden where we are safe to explore, learn and create for God.

When we are young and fall in love, we often enter into this kind of union without being fully conscious of the responsibility and sacred tasks asked of us. We just want someone else to make us happy, someone else to make us feel valuable, and someone else to tell us we are beautiful, handsome, smart and sexy and affirm our worth.

We also too easily let go of the other sacred relationships with friends, service organizations, family members and co-workers that feed us in an entirely different way. This leaves us vulnerable and isolated if and when that relationship is over.

A romantic relationship is an opportunity to collaborate with another person to manifest the glory of spirit here on Earth. To enter the relationship fully, there must be a certain level of awareness about who you are and what you offer. No delusions. Both people choose to show up entirely ready to work the garden. One of you may have to remind the other that the garden needs some pruning and weeding. But the garden stays tended.

But let there be spaces in your togetherness and let the winds of the heavens dance between you.

Love one another but make not a bond of love: Let it rather be a moving sea between the shores of your souls.

~ Kahil Gibran

I have met countless couples in which one party is more invested in maintaining the relationship than the other. That person feels resentful and bitter, and the other party feels harassed or apathetic. If one person just wants to take from the garden and has no desire to get hands dirty and commit time to create this beautiful space, the relationship will not last. That however, might be the lesson. If it is, move on.

Often, we want a relationship to last forever and focus so hard on forever that we do not enjoy moments we are experiencing. The old adage that some people come into our lives for a reason, a season or a lifetime applies in romantic love.

Many married couples grow a romantic, sacred garden and then assume it will take care of itself. Even more couples stop nurturing it when children enter the picture. This is easy to do. The love we have for our children is unconditional, so it's easy to turn our attention to our children, even into their twenties and thirties. This does not serve our children either.

If one person is just stopping into the garden, taking what he or she needs and leaving the other gardener to do all the work, the hard-working partner begins asking if the relationship is worth it.

We hold on to dysfunctional relationships not because they are serving us or the other person, but because of our fragile egos. What if the other person leaves and finds another person to love? Does that mean we are not loveable? What if we let go of this relationship and never find another? What will other people think?

When we really love someone else, we recognize that he or she is never ours to possess. Not being with us might be exactly what is needed to serve a higher purpose. Letting someone go with grace is an act of surrender, opening our hearts for greater blessing and God's plan.

When a marriage ends and if and when you are ready to begin dating again, I would like to suggest you consider some of the dating tips that follow. But please consider nurturing the relationship you have with yourself and God first. It will give you greater vision and clarity when meeting new people.

These little nuggets of wisdom have been acquired from my personal experiences but also from dear friends I admire.

They come from five years of group discussions with divorcés and divorcées of various ages. Their insights and wisdom have been blessings to me, and I share their wisdom with you.

1. Explore your readiness. Do not let anyone tell you when you are ready to re-enter the dating world. Take your time, and get to know who you are and what you love, and you will know when you are ready.

2. Be honest on your profile if you are Internet dating. I hear time and time again, the most frustrating thing about Internet dating is that people are dishonest. Well, some people are, but you do not have to be. All your actions should stem from your values, including how you portray yourself.

3. Be honest within the new relationship. If you want to experience an authentic relationship and build on a solid foundation of trust and respect, you too must be honest. Do not lie about your age, how many times you've been

married, and so on. I am not suggesting you tell your new romantic interest every sordid detail, but the basics should be honest. Moving forward, you should remain honest about feelings and situations that arise.

4. No gender bashing, please. If we have unresolved issues around our exes or men or women in general, we may feel justified to point out the flaws of the opposite sex, or the same sex if we are gay. We do so and then can't understand why we attract dysfunctional, unhealthy situations. Gender bashing is a turnoff and not sexy at all. Get over it to get on with it.

5. Don't act desperate. Remember, you are a beloved child of God. You are worthy and have value. Enter each dating situation from this place, and do not put on a false persona. Hold steady, remember who you are, and enter each relationship curious and open but not attached to the outcome. Too much texting, e-mailing and calling can be a burden to someone who has a full life. You can use these forms of communication for expressions of love, but get together in person, and when you are apart, focus on your life.

6. Have the conversation. You are a grown-up, and if you can't discuss sex with another adult you shouldn't be having it. If you feel pressured in any way, talk about it and set up some white picket fence boundaries if needed. If you are willing to share your beautiful body with another, you should be able to discuss concerns, such as sexually transmitted diseases, monogamy, or any other concern you may have about this sacred act.

7.   Listen. It can be so exciting to finally meet someone that you forget to listen with not only your ears but your heart and higher self. Trust your intuition. Do not go full speed ahead if you have inklings that something is not right. If you feel excited, passionate and filled with love, still stay alert as you move along. Are you perhaps bringing your old habits and patterns from your past relationships? Are they muddying up the new one? When you really listen, you work from the higher self, allowing for a deeper experience.

8.   Be present. Don't worry about where the relationship is going or if you are going to need a pre-nup. Don't worry about whether you will have another date. When you do this, you are acting from fear, and fear attracts more fear-based thoughts. Love the time you are sharing, and if you don't, don't be there. Enjoy the moments for what they are. Show up as yourself, the best version of you. Don't try to be anyone else, including what you might have been 20 years ago. You, right now, are sexy, attractive, and perfect. That is the gift you will bring to the new relationship. Enjoy yourself.

Dear Lord,

*I am deserving of all the beauty
and love you provide for me ~*

*I release the fear in my heart and
in its place create a space
to receive love in all forms ~*

*As I am filled with love, I give
love to others with ease
and grace ~*

Thank you, God, for this moment ~

It is perfect ~

Amen . . . I'm in.

Week Eight

Questions and Divine Assignments

Age does not protect you from love. But love, to some extent, protects you from age.

~ Anais Nin

Why is it important to recognize and honor love in its different forms?

Beth Tiger

What are some things you can do to bring more love into your daily life?

Are you ready for a romantic relationship? If so, why? If not, why not?

Are you clear about who you are and what you offer others?

Do you love and appreciate yourself as you are, right this minute?

Action: List ten things you love about yourself.

1.

2.

3.

4.

5.

6.

7.

8.

9.

10.

How many of those things are superficial?

List ten things you would love in a partnership, not in someone in particular.

1.

2.

3.

4.

5.

6.

7.

8.

9.

10.

How do each of these help you advance toward a more service-oriented, spiritually aligned life?

Chapter 8

Discovering Our Passions

Defining Our Purpose and Creating Support

When you are inspired by some great purpose, some extraordinary project, all your thoughts break their bonds: Your mind transcends limitations, your consciousness expands in every direction, and you find yourself in a new, great, and wonderful world. Dormant forces, faculties and talents become alive, and your discover yourself to be a greater person by far than you ever dreamed yourself to be.

~ Patanjali

Let's begin with an affirmation:

My life is a journey. I am allowed to change my mind, make mistakes and begin anew. Each choice I make is aligned with my values and goals for today.

Welcome to Week Eight, our final week together during this process. I applaud you already for getting here. The past few weeks, I have asked a lot of you, and I hope that you have really stretched those muscles of self-love, forgiveness and surrender.

This week is all about exploring your passions, naming your soul's purpose and considering how you can create a support network that is "pro you"!

You have already received many tools that help unearth what may be lying dormant deep inside the depths of your being—your passion. You are able to identify your feelings both emotionally and physically; you are more in touch with what you value about yourself, others and this world; you are tapped into spirit; and you are in the throes of a juicy love affair, with yourself.

If you don't feel as though you are there on all these levels yet, that is OK. Remember what I wrote at the beginning of this book. Everything you need for a fulfilling, deeply satisfying, love-filled life exists within you already. You are perfect just the way you are. The concepts and suggestions in this book are merely tools to help you awaken from the dream and get you back in touch with your powers of creation.

Finding the right work is like discovering your own soul in the world.

~ Thomas Moore

Passion is energy, and when we feel passionately about something, the feelings it evokes can be intense. We may feel love, lust, anger, sadness or rage. The feelings take many forms, but passion itself is just energy. It is what we do with passion that matters.

When you see and hear an infant's crying, it's clear that baby is pretty passionate about its emotional state. My children, as babies and toddlers, would turn bright red, break into sweats and clench their fists. Tears would stream down their faces. In an attempt to quiet them, I admit, I often tried to stifle their passion.

We do not always know what to do with a child's enthusiasm and passion, even when it is positive. We often convey, as a reflex, that we'd like him or her to quiet down, lower the vibration, be still, go to sleep—in other words, act in a widely acceptable manner.

In our modern culture, we are so afraid to feel passionately that many of us are numbed completely to our feelings by prescription drugs. Many of us fear that what we are feeling is "too much" or too negative. Why do we feel this way? What if we allowed ourselves to feel passionately about ourselves, our children, our lives? Perhaps we would no longer tolerate half the nonsense we do.

Feeling passionately about something indicates that it is affecting a core value. So instead of trying to avoid or deny the feeling, examine it and how it makes you feel; then use it to help you make choices that support your well-being.

Finding our passions, however, is a different concept. Identifying what we are passionate about helps us understand why we are on this planet in service to God.

I know that each human being has a unique purpose. There are no accidents, and if you are here, you are meant to be here. I hope the work you have been doing these past seven weeks has stripped away some of your excuses for not finding out what that purpose is.

This week, by examining what you are passionate about, you will be able to name your purpose and begin to honor it.

Of course, you may choose to hold back a while longer, and that is OK too. You will get to your soul's destiny sooner or later. I just hope you remember the old Grand Canyon metaphor. It is my prayer that you choose to walk through the doors of destiny rather than be shoved.

All human actions have one or more of these seven causes: chance, nature, compulsions, habit, reason, passion, desire.

~ Aristotle

You have a purpose. It's as if before we incarnated into being, each soul chose a purpose to fulfill for God. For some, the purpose is to teach, for others it is to heal, for others it is to inspire. Only you know for sure what yours is.

However, our purpose is not so elusive that we can only hope to understand it. Most of us have been living in alignment with our purpose for our entire lives; we were just not fully aware which choices were not reflective of it.

Trust me, for many of you, it is staring you right in the face. For years, I prayed to God to reveal my purpose. I did past-life regressions; I did psychic readings, energy work, meditation, you name it. Then one day, it hit me. I was straightening up after one of the Flying Solo sessions, and a small group lingered to share phone numbers and offer quiet words of encouragement to one another.

I was buzzing as I observed them.

I finally realized that my soul's purpose was to create community from a place of love and tolerance for all. Now, I know that sounds awfully grand, but really it is very basic. As I began looking back over my life, I was surprised to see that creating community was something I had been doing all along, just not always with eyes wide open and a heart filled with love.

I love having friends over, and I enjoy seeing my friends talking with one another, not only sharing with me. I love sharing my vacation home with family and friends and watching them as they try something new with their loved ones.

My brother and I rekindled an extended family tradition and began holding a family reunion each summer. I can't tell you how happy it makes me to see familiar faces as I pull up to our little hotel in upstate New York each summer.

Watching my children run off and get into trouble with their second and third cousins gives me a deep sense of fulfillment. It was through this type of reflection that I could see that my purpose and what drives me on a daily basis were one in the same.

I knew at last that my purpose and commitment to God were larger than just throwing parties and networking. I realized that the other element to my purpose was creating a space or a community where each person who took part felt safe and inspired to connect with the Source. Do you see where I am going with this?

Your passions, where you are called to be of service, how you feel emotionally, what you value and cherish and ultimately what motivates you are linked to your soul's purpose. As you grow and evolve, the purpose will too, but the keystones will remain the same.

Passion rebuilds the world for the youth. It makes all things alive and significant.

~ Ralph Waldo Emerson

Knowing what your purpose is and what makes you feel passionately are important elements in creating right relationships in your life. For instance, if you are passionate about animals, could you imagine living your entire life in a home with no pets? If you are passionate about travel, can you imagine living with someone who only enjoys staying home? Or what if your soul's purpose is to be mother or father to many people, including unwanted children in our world? Imagine sharing a life with someone who was most content with no children. One or both of you would have to make a huge value compromise and deny his or her purpose and unique promise to God.

Much of the time, we deny our passions as well as our divine purpose in the most insidious way. This comes from apathy, fear, numbness and a disconnection from the Divine. We get so caught up resisting change that we allow ourselves to become stagnant. Pieces of us begin to die.

We become those little children who are told to hush, settle down and cut it out. Acting like ladies, being gentlemen, and lowering our vibrations cause so many of us to fall out of touch with our true natures.

Today is the day to get excited about the life that is yours. Live from a place of passion, love, gratitude, surrender and service, and hear the Still Small Voice within. It is SCREAMING to be acknowledged.

If we did all the things we are capable of, we would literally astound ourselves.

~ Thomas A. Edison

At the end of this chapter I am giving you a series of juicy questions meant to inspire you and help you dream of the life you will create with the help of God. Enjoy these questions, and in the future, think back on them and see if your actions and desires match up.

Remember, when you are consciously living your life, tapped into the Source and living your purpose, you will know it with every fiber of your being. It will feel right, and this adjustment will not feel hard. It will give you a sense of accomplishment, joy and delight.

I long to accomplish a great and noble task, but it is my chief duty to accomplish small tasks as if they were great and noble

~ Helen Keller

When I facilitate a group and witness their compassion and friendship, along with the empowered changes they make, it is so deeply gratifying that I feel blessed and enriched. That's when I know I am "on purpose" and doing God's work. When I do something that makes me irate and I complain, I know it is time to reevaluate how this is serving me or anyone else. You cannot change anyone but yourself. So keep the focus on you.

Passions are fun, and we are meant to have fun! I get to experience being Beth Tiger. No one else does, and I am determined to have many laughs, dance as much as possible, create as many positive experiences as I can and beautify as much as possible for my Lord. It is my job, and it is yours too. We are here to create heaven on Earth. Let's get to it.

Now that you are divorced, take this unique time to discover what it is that you feel passionate about. Do you love art? Do you enjoy theater? Make a plan to take your hottest date, yourself, to an art show or a play; you have no one else to please but you.

Perhaps you want to try creating art yourself or writing your memoirs or a screenplay. I don't want to throw out too many ideas, as I want this to be all about you and what you love. But I know that many of you have spent your time focusing on the needs of spouses or children. Now, even if you have young children, it is the time to figure your passions out.

You owe it to your children. You will give them permission to do the same. We can only lead by example. We must walk the walk.

Passion is the genesis of genius.

~ Tony Robbins

As we begin to explore passions and purpose, it is also time to consider the people and situations we are around. So many times, we go to a dry well for water again and again and are surprised when our thirst is not quenched. Instead, we feel drained of energy. How do we expect to make lasting changes if we sabotage our growth with energy-depleting experiences? There is nothing loving about staying in friendships and other relationships that are not serving our or the other person's best life.

My support network is the fabric that holds my material life in place. It consists of God and the people and institutions that support me and my attempts to live well.

When I got divorced, I realized I was not careful or conscious about how I created my prior network, and I was lax about who was part of it. I had to evaluate a few things with an open, loving and forgiving heart and release some people and situations that were no longer serving them or me. This does not have to be done overnight.

Now, more than ever, you need a strong support network. Why is it important to be especially aware of your choices for support at this stage? Let's look at a fictional example.

Debbie was married to her husband for 10 years; they had three gorgeous children. After her first child was born, Debbie was consumed with her family. It was exhausting, but she did a fantastic job with not only her firstborn, but the other two children that followed.

When Debbie got married, she was very close with many girlfriends, but as her life evolved with her children she lost touch with her old friends and made new friends through her children's activities. She lived in a large home in an affluent town. Debbie loved her lifestyle, but inside she was deeply dissatisfied with herself and her marriage. On the outside, it looked as though Debbie had it all: many friends, many social activities. However, inside, Debbie yearned for more, and she was extremely lonely. Her husband was working very hard to support their family, and he and she were growing apart.

Debbie had little time for the church community she was involved in heavily prior to marriage. She went to church only on major holidays and for the Mommy and Me group once a month. It seemed that all of her current associations were either because of her children or from her husband's business dealings. Debbie's family lived across the country, so she felt detached from and unsupported by them.

When she went through her divorce, her soon-to-be ex-husband paid for her high-powered attorney and her expenses. After her divorce, she had to liquidate their joint assets, including their large home, and Debbie moved into a smaller three-bedroom home in a new town.

Debbie appreciated all that she had and worked hard with a therapist to heal herself during this process. She was focused on her children and her new job. She hated her new job though, and she felt bitter that she had to work there just to survive. When the kids were with her ex, she found the weekends to be long and depressing.

At one point shortly after her divorce, she had a financial issue that needed addressing, and when she called her accountant, she could not believe what the fees were. These costs were something she never paid attention to in the past. So once again, she felt scared and unsupported.

At this low point, she was encouraged by her therapist to attend a divorce support group, and when she did, she saw she was not alone. She started making new friends and going out occasionally.

One afternoon, she was driving home from her divorce support meeting and noticed a group of people leaving a church. She decided to stop and get a schedule. It was an interfaith church, which really resonated with her new outlook, so the next Sunday she brought her children to the service.

She loved it and felt awakened for the first time in a many years. There was a coffee social afterward, and she met some new people, as did her children.

She was also encouraged by her divorce group to seek financial and legal help from a nonprofit organization in her county. Debbie would never have thought of this, as she and her husband had always had the money to pay top lawyers, accountants and advisers.

Debbie finally realized that she would either have to show up 100 percent in her new life, including her job, or she would never move forward. At work, she found ways to give joy and make new friendships, even if the work itself was not her favorite.

After being divorced for almost two hard years, Debbie was excitedly walking out the door of her home, heading off to a weekend getaway with girlfriends she had made in her support group. Her new life looked totally different from her past life. It was so much more authentic in its design. It was then that she acknowledged that her life was perfect because she had designed it herself, a little at time, with consideration, acceptance and love. She was grateful.

All our dreams can come true, if we have the courage to pursue them.

~ Walt Disney

When you divorce, you often lose so many other relationships that you feel isolated and lonely. But you do not have to be. You should be satisfied with keeping your own company, but it is also necessary to create a pro-you network and to do so knowing what you value and feel passionately about. It is also critical that you know how to say no to situations and relationships that are not good for you.

A pro-you network should not only contain great friendships, but may also include a wonderful lawyer, an honest accountant, a compassionate doctor, a spiritual mentor, a financial adviser, an insurance agent, a few reliable babysitters if you have young children, a pet sitter and vet if you have pets, handy people and house care help if needed and perhaps even a therapist or coach. Remember, we are interdependent, and at this stage in your life, you have the opportunity to decide who will be included in the next chapter and what roles they will play.

Today, choose to live from a place of passion and purpose with a servant's heart doing God's will.

Phew . . . that was a mouthful. But it's a solid prescription for peace, joy and right relationships.

Dear Lord,

I am excited about the day before me ~

*I honor all the talents and gifts
you have so generously
given to me ~*

*I commit to you that I will use my
passionate energy, inspiration, talents
and gifts to create a better world ~*

Amen . . . I'm in.

Week Eight

Questions and Divine Assignments

If one advances confidently in the direction of his dreams, and endeavors to live the life which he has imagined, he will meet with success unexpected in common hours.

~ Henry David Thoreau

Who are the closest people in your life?

Do they serve you and you them? Or are any of these relationships in need of repair, white picket fence boundaries or release?

If you need to end a relationship, how can you do so with love?

What are some ways that you can create a more pro-you network?

When you were a little child, what did you know for sure you would do when you grew up?

How is that the same or different from what your life looks like?

What would you do if you knew you could not fail?

What would you do if money were no object?

What do you fantasize about when you are doing housework, driving, taking a bath?

What would you regret not doing if your life ended now?

All of this week's questions are for your use to create a map for personal exploration and unearthing what moves you and makes you feel inspired and passionate.

Action: Take a meaningful risk. Is there something you have dreamed of doing but have been too afraid to do? It does not have to be jumping from a plane with a parachute, but it does have to be something that stretches you emotionally. When you face your fears with a positive action, you raise your energy and affirm YES to the universe. It expands your comfort zone, even if the outcome is not what you might expect.

Taking the risk is the win!

Chapter 9

Ready to Soar!

The Lord will guide you continually

and satisfy your needs in parched places . . .

and you shall be like a well-watered garden . . .

whose waters do not fail.

~ Isaiah 58:11 (esv)

We are ending our journey together, but you are embarking on a beautiful new chapter in your life. I want to take this moment to remind you of a simple yet profound teaching.

YOU ARE AND HAVE ALWAYS BEEN A PERFECT EXPRESSION OF GOD.

All that you will ever need exists inside of you, and each time you learn something, you are technically awakening pieces of the truth that are within. The information in this book is a guide meant to inspire or light what is already living inside of you.

It is my absolute belief that each person is a perfect manifestation of God. It is our flaws that give others the ability to see us shimmer when light is shown upon us. It is also these flaws and painful experiences that give us the compassion and grace needed to be a servant to mankind, which is life's true work.

I hold no authority over what might work for you, so sit in your knowing. Discard what is not personal truth. Stash the learning in your toolbox, and keep it close.

As the final exercise in this workbook, I want to encourage you to write a Flying Solo mission statement as a renewed being, capable of standing on your own. Acknowledge what YOU know for sure about yourself, at this moment, having survived the trauma of separation and divorce. I also ask that you include what you are committed to achieving with God, now that you know better.

Take one week to do this, enjoy the process, and feel excited about the year before you. Once you are done, place your statement in an envelope, seal it, and address it to yourself. Either stick it inside a calendar and mail it to yourself in one year, or ask a fellow traveler on the Flying Solo journey to mail it to you a year from now.

Remember to stay connected to those who feed your soul. No going to the dry well for water. I encourage you to check out my Facebook page and stay in touch with the Flying Solo community by sharing anecdotes, "wins" and stories of inspiration with others who are going through the process. I believe it takes a village to raise us all up, so find one or create one.

Finally, on the following pages I would like to share some great books, online sites, and places to nurture and nourish the soul. I am the owner of A Life Well Lived, but I have no affiliation with any of the other resources listed. I simply offer them to you because each one has helped me along my personal journey.

Today choose to live your life inspired & on purpose. You are the author of this chapter, make it your best.

May God bless you today & always ~ Beth Tiger

Resource Guide

Transformational books from my personal bookshelf

29 Gifts ~ Cami Walker

A Course in Miracles ~ Foundation for Inner Peace

A Return to Love ~ Marianne Williamson

Excuses Begone! ~ Dr. Wayne Dyer

Feel the Fear and Do It Anyway ~ Susan Jeffers

Return of the Bird Tribes ~ Ken Carey

Spiritual Divorce ~ Debbie Ford

The Shack ~ William P. Young

The Source of Miracles ~ Kathleen McGowan

You Can Heal Your Life ~ Louise Hay

Places to nurture the soul and grow

A Life Well Lived ~ www.alifewelllived.com

Canyon Ranch ~ www.canyonranch.com

Esalen ~ www.esalen.org/

Kripalu Center ~ www.kripalu.org

Miraval Resort ~ www.miravalresorts.com

Omega Institute ~ www.eomega.org

Sacred France Tours ~ www.sacredfrance.com

Internet resources

A Course in Miracles
www.acim.org

Beliefnet
www.beliefnet.com

Daily OM
www.dailyom.com

TUT's Adventurers Club
www.tut.com

Unity
www.unity.org

Dear Lord,

*I bless and release my ex-spouse
into your loving care.*

Please give him/her joy and peace ~

*I honor and give thanks for all I learned
and experienced within that relationship ~*

*Today I am open to all that you
have planned for me ~*

I greet each person with a loving heart ~

*Today I choose to think thoughts
filled with abundance
and gratitude ~*

*Please gently guide me back on
course when I waiver ~*

Amen . . . I'm in.

Dear Lord,

*Today is a new day, filled
with promise and hope ~*

*I have earned these wings, and
it is my time to soar ~*

*Through faith, I step off the edge, knowing
that God is my partner and all is well ~*

*I fly freely and with ease as a
perfect expression of spirit
and inspire others to do the same ~*

For this I give thanks ~

Amen . . . I'm in!

The moving cover image, "Phoenix Rising from the Ashes," and the Flying Solo wing were created by New Jersey tattoo artist Scotty Lowe. Scotty lives with his wife and two daughters in Butler, New Jersey. He has a BFA from Ohio State University and an MFA from the City College of New York. Scotty has been a tattoo artist for 21 years at Shotsie's Tattoo in Wayne, New Jersey.

CPSIA information can be obtained at www.ICGtesting.com
Printed in the USA
BVOW071209090512

289715BV00002B/3/P

9 781452 546155